PRAISE FOR
THE POWER OF WOW

"A must-read about an extraordinary business endeavor in our everyday world. Tony and company have pioneered how to scale organizational effectiveness with heart, and much of their story is shared here with transparency, humility, and great storytelling. This provides a glimpse of the future of how to get things done on the planet, sustainably, with efficient elegance."

— *David Allen, author of* Getting Things Done:
The Art of Stress-Free Productivity

Customers will never love a company until the employees love it first, and Zappos proves it. Lots of CEOs love to write books to tell us how great their companies are; what a treat to hear the stories from the actual employees who work there.

—*Simon Sinek, optimist and* New York Times *bestselling author of* Start with Why *and* Leaders Eat Last

"Zappos is a powerful example of a modern company that has embraced a simple truth: Passionate employees are any organization's single greatest asset. *The Power of WOW* is a timely reminder that no business leader can afford to ignore the value of an inspired workforce."

— *Chip Conley, hospitality entrepreneur and author of* Wisdom at Work

The Power of WOW offers the wisdom of the collective: a direct glimpse into the thinkers, dreamers, and doers that bring Zappos to life every day. This collection of stories will fuel a passion that you can bring back to your business and take your own culture to the next level."

— *BJ Bueno, founder of The Cult Branding Company*

"Over the past decade, I've had the privilege of training thousands of Zappos employees. What a remarkable and resilient company. The highly personal stories and lessons in this book should be read by all modern business leaders—and anyone who wants to make customers and employees alike say WOW!"

— Dr. Sean Stephenson, professional speaker
  and author of Get Off Your "But"

"In today's world, there is a massive gap between perception and reality, highlighted particularly by social media. So when you look at a prolific and aspirational company like Zappos through this lens, you have to wonder . . . is this distorted hype or reality?

The Power of WOW gives a glimpse into the humanity that drives Zappos—real people navigating the corporate landscape of a visionary company that truly walks the walk. This book showcases the vulnerability, the realities, and the highs and lows of an aspirational human company, building upon its foundation—people first.

The Power of WOW is not a social-hype piece, but a reinforcement that its perception and its reality are in fact, one and the same."

— Mick Ebeling, founder and CEO of Not Impossible Labs

"Zapponians work like great artists, communicate like good family, and laugh like a bunch of people partying their asses off in Vegas. And I love them for that. So go read this book, you won't regret it."

— Joseph Gordon-Levitt, actor and founder
  of HITRECORD

THE POWER OF WOW

THE POWER OF WOW

OF

WOW

*How to Electrify
Your Work and Your Life by
Putting Service First*

From the **Employees of Zappos** as told to
#1 *New York Times*–bestselling coauthor **Mark Dagostino**

BenBella Books, Inc.
Dallas, TX

BenBella

BenBella Books, Inc.
10440 N. Central Expressway, Suite 800
Dallas, TX 75231
www.benbellabooks.com
Send feedback to feedback@benbellabooks.com

Printed in the United States of America
10 9 8 7 6 5 4 3 2 1

Library of Congress Control Number: 2019015086
ISBN 9781948836579 (trade cloth)
ISBN 9781948836821 (electronic)

33614081529199

Copyediting by Elizabeth Degenhard
Proofreading by Sarah Vostok and Chris Gage
Text design and composition by Kit Sweeney Photography & Design
Employee headshots by Peter Gaunt
Cover photo © Design Assets
Cover design and photo editing by Derrin Hawkins and Sarah Avinger
Printed by Lake Book Manufacturing

Distributed to the trade by Two Rivers Distribution, an Ingram brand
www.tworiversdistribution.com

This book is dedicated to all of our customers, employees, community members, vendors, and shareholders that have been a part of our journey over the past twenty years (and for many more to come).

Zappos Company Purpose:

<u>To inspire the world</u> by showing it's possible to simultaneously deliver happiness to customers, employees, community, vendors, and shareholders in a <u>long-term, sustainable way</u>.

tl;dr—To live and deliver WOW

CONTENTS

WELCOME

Rather than write a traditional foreword here at the beginning, I decided to sprinkle random color commentary throughout the book instead. You'll see my comments in thought bubbles like the one you're reading right now. Think of these as text messages I'm sending you at various points in the book.

In addition to all the Zappos employees who contributed to this book, we partnered with Mark Dagostino, the #1 New York Times bestselling author of various books, including The Magnolia Story, *to interview us, write, and help weave all of our stories together.*

Without further ado, let's start with Mark's story of how this whole project came to life . . .

—Tony Hsieh
CEO, Zappos.com

INTRODUCTION:
A HIGHER PURPOSE

Ten years ago—coincidentally, right around the same time Zappos was finalizing its partnership deal with a little company called Amazon—I published my very first book, *My Life Outside the Ring*, with legendary wrestler Hulk Hogan.

I wrote that book while juggling a relentlessly busy, more-than-full-time day job at one of the biggest magazines in the world with my family duties of helping to raise two young children. Which means I wrote it in my "spare time," toiling away at my laptop from midnight to 3 A.M., every day.

It was exhausting. It was invigorating. It was challenging. It took a toll on my family and my sleep—but the effort paid off. My first book became a *New York Times* bestseller and would eventually serve as the launch pad for the biggest, most daring decision of my adult life: to leave my steady job behind and take on the life of a full-time coauthor; a life of working from home, doing what I love, but never knowing where my next paycheck might come from.

My leap of faith worked pretty well at first. In my first few years I wrote books with a US presidential candidate, a legendary sports figure, an army general, TV stars, and more. I loved what I was doing—but something was off. As time went by, some of these books weren't selling as well as I'd hoped. After more than half a decade, I was just sort of getting by (financially speaking). And I was starting to question whether I'd made a bad decision, mostly because the potential new book projects that kept coming my way seemed increasingly driven by less-than-thrilling subjects. They were ego-driven projects by businesspeople who wanted to capitalize on my prior successes, or books from celebrities who wanted to entertain with gossip and fun stories (and not much else) to make some money.

Those sorts of books *may* have filled up my bank account just fine, but as I considered whether or not to take them, I realized they did nothing to fill my heart and soul. They felt shallow. They felt like something less than what I ought to be dedicating my life to creating.

What I loved most about writing books, and what I tried to infuse into every book I had tackled so far, was coaxing out the best, most inspirational stories from my subjects. I loved finding out how these everyday people actually made it to the top. How they overcame obstacles. How they rose above challenges to chase and achieve their goals.

So I made a decision: I *only* wanted to write books that inspire—the kind of books that make people wake up in the morning and go out and chase their dreams. I want to dedicate myself to writing books that remind people that the world is full of amazing possibilities, and that all of us have a chance to make life better for ourselves and others every day.

To follow through on that commitment, I chose to back out of a potentially lucrative book deal that didn't serve that purpose.

Was I nervous to let go of a project that was already in process? Yes. Did I know where my next paycheck would come from? No. But I knew it was the right thing to do. So I did it.

It was a leap of faith—the same sort of leap that businesses like Zappos have to sometimes take when they want to transition from good to great.

As fate would have it, just a few weeks later I got a call about a book project that struck me as having the potential to live up to my new goal. So I chased it. I gave it my all. I flew all the way from New Hampshire to the middle of Texas for a fifteen-minute pitch meeting, and, in that meeting, while listening to this couple's goals for their book, I mentioned my big decision: "I only want to work on books that inspire." I shared a bit about my personal journey, and they shared a bit about theirs. Despite our geographic differences, it seemed we had a lot in common. We'd all been through some struggles, and we were able to laugh about those similarities. Before we knew it, our meeting had gone well over an hour.

This couple was in a position to hire just about any writer in the world to write their book. But they chose me. And I'm positive that my decision to focus on inspiring others was a big part of the reason they did so.

Those people were Chip and Joanna Gaines, the stars of the HGTV show *Fixer Upper*, and our book, *The Magnolia Story*, would go on to become a runaway #1 *New York Times* bestseller. It sold more than a million copies in its first three months, and more than two years after its initial publication, it still managed to climb back onto some bestseller lists during the holiday shopping season. It's still selling in hardcover to this day.

The amazing thing is that it wasn't a fluke. I've coauthored three other books that have hit the *New York Times* bestseller list since then, and every one of them has adhered to the same set of inspirational values I purposefully set out to follow. Putting my focus on something bigger than myself, something bigger than just earning a paycheck, paid off. And the simple act of focusing my life's work on serving a higher purpose improved my personal life as well, in more ways than I can possibly relate in this short introduction.

So you might understand why I was a little skeptical when someone named Kelly Smith contacted me (through the link on my less-than-fancy, $1-per-month website) saying she wanted to talk about writing a book for Zappos. *Why would I be interested in taking on a business book, which I assumed would be a "corporate" project, after I'd left the corporate world far behind and made this big decision to focus on inspiration?*

If you know what Zappos is all about, you're probably laughing at my naïveté. To be honest, I didn't know very much about Zappos.

I didn't know anything about Mark, so we're even.

Tony

I knew they sold shoes, but I had never ordered anything from their website. I knew of Zappos CEO Tony Hsieh and that he'd written a book himself, but I hadn't read it. Still, there was something about Kelly's initial email that caught my eye: She said she wanted to create a book told in the diverse voices of the company's own employees, which intrigued me. I'd read plenty of business books and I had written plenty of business articles in my career as a journalist (especially during my early years at the *Boston Globe*), but I had never seen a business book written that way. It felt new to me. It felt unique. I wanted to hear more, so I set up a call with her team.

In the first hour of what would become a two-year journey into the heart of Zappos' culture, I realized that what Zappos was doing wasn't about selling shoes. It wasn't even about "business," in the traditional sense. It was about service. It was about innovation. It was about reimagining what a business could be and how a business could survive for the long term, while making not only its customers but its employees, its shareholders, its community—everyone—happier in the process.

I traveled to Zappos' headquarters in Las Vegas and spent time with its employees. I sat around a campfire with Tony Hsieh and steeped myself in this culture, and I quickly realized that this experience wasn't just about writing a book. This experience was inspiring *me* to want to do even bigger and better things with my own life's work, which is exactly what Zappos aims to do with all of its interactions: This company's very real goal is to change the way business is done, and to inspire other businesses, big and small, to do something more innovative, and more *inspirational*, along the way.

That doesn't even sound real, right? In this cynical world in which we live, it's easy to dismiss earnest integrity and a desire to do good as some sort of a marketing gimmick. But I was blown away to find that every employee I met at Zappos had a story to tell that backed up the company mission. It didn't matter if it was someone in a leadership position, or behind the front desk, or driving me in a Zappos-branded shuttle to the airport. Every employee had their own passionate, personal story to share, mostly about how changing the way they work has changed their lives for the better. And each of them very clearly showed that their goal in sharing these stories with me wasn't to self-aggrandize—it was to inspire others to take a fresh look at what *they* do and to consider ways to make *their* lives and *their* work better, too.

I realize that this isn't news to all of you. Some of you who've picked up this book are already steeped in the Zappos mystique. You likely know far more about Zappos than I did when I first started working on this project. But while I had to play catch-up (first and foremost by devouring Tony Hsieh's book *Delivering Happiness*), what I've learned on my journey with this company so far is that anything anyone thinks they know about Zappos, whether from past books or various articles that have appeared in the press, barely scratches the surface.

What you're about to read in this book is the result of *ten additional years'* worth of collected experience, data, and information to back up what was still mostly hypothesis and dreams back in 2009. The WOW culture, the Core Values, and the dedication to "profits, passion, and purpose" that Zappos became known for in the past still apply, but now those concepts have been road tested over and over. And as you'll soon see, while a few of Zappos' ideas haven't worked, every failure has been a lesson on a road to an exciting future.

Today, the goals at Zappos are bigger than they've ever been, as stated in the company purpose: **To inspire the world by showing it's possible to simultaneously deliver happiness to customers, employees, community, vendors, and shareholders in a long-term, sustainable way.**

That may sound lofty, but Zappos is in the unique position to set lofty goals—and then chase them. While they have the backing and resources of Amazon, the deal Tony signed back in 2009 ensures that the company remains independent and autonomous.

> In fact, Amazon and Zappos have an internal document titled The 5 Tenets Document, which says:
>
> 1. Zappos will operate independently, overseen by a management committee that will function similar to the prior Zappos board of directors. The committee will initially be made up of three people from Amazon and three people from Zappos.
> 2. Zappos' unique culture has been core to its success to date, and we look to protect it. . . .

Tony

Which means that as long as it's delivering profits and growth, Zappos has the freedom to do, basically, whatever it wants. And what Zappos has become in the second decade of its existence is much more than an online retailer, and even more than a WOW-worthy service company: Zappos has become an incubator for new ideas; a testing ground for the future of how companies large and small can adapt, grow, and thrive in the face of an exponentially increasing rate of change.

The ultimate goal is to deliver WOW to everyone. To create a business formula in which there are no losers. To turn Zappos into a self-organizing, ever-changing, dynamic system that delivers wins for all parties involved: employees, customers, shareholders, vendors, community, the world—*everyone*.

And that is no easy feat.

As you're about to discover, the company has gone through some pretty crazy ups and downs in the last decade while trying to enact and establish a way of doing business that hasn't been put into practice at scale before. But what Zappos is aiming toward, and what it's unleashing, is a self-organized workplace in which employees operate with the same autonomy and ability to innovate as Zappos itself does under the Amazon umbrella.

TONY

What will that look like?

You're about to find out.

To best explain all of this, it's time for me to get out of the way and to hand this book over to those employees. After all, this book was their idea, and allowing them to pull back the curtain themselves is the best way of not only explaining but actually showing you what Zappos is up to. *They'll* tell you the story of how Zappos operates, how they got here, and how much fun work can be (for entry-level employees and CEOs alike) when work comes from a place of connection and service. They'll explain how trust and service in the workplace leads to an unleashing of creativity. And they'll also share where Zappos (and maybe the rest of the business world) is headed next, using examples of how staying true to a culture and giving employees the ability to lead through self-organization and Market-Based Dynamics (MBD) is already creating new experiences, new categories, and new profitability in areas that no one at Zappos could have imagined when they first got started.

Whether you consider yourself a leader, a follower, an entrepreneur, a civil servant, a homebody, or a couch potato; whoever you are, wherever you are in work or in life, I hope you'll find that this book is written in service to you. Because it truly comes from the heart, from all of the Zappos employees you're about to meet. And my greatest hope, *their* greatest hope, is that this peek into the ever-unfolding story of Zappos will WOW you—so you'll be inspired to go out and WOW the world, too.

—Mark Dagostino

PART
I

Connecting

THE HEART OF THE SERVICE-MINDED CULTURE

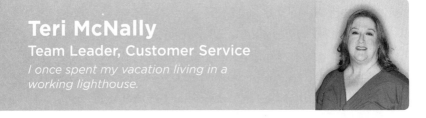

Teri McNally
Team Leader, Customer Service
I once spent my vacation living in a working lighthouse.

It's amazing how opening your heart changes everything.

In this case, it all started with a phone call.

"Hello?"

"Hi, this is Teri calling from Zappos.com. Is this Susan?"

"Yes, it is."

"Hi, Susan. I believe you called into our Customer Loyalty department yesterday to let us know that most of your shoe order didn't arrive on time as promised."

"Yes."

"I just wanted to call back to let you know that I reviewed that call, and I'm just so sorry for everything you and your family are going through."

"I . . . thank you. Is there another problem with my order?"

"No, no. The rest of the shoes will arrive tomorrow. I triple-checked that they're en route before I called you, so I just wanted to let you know that they're definitely on the way, and I also wanted to apologize that we didn't do more for you when you called in yesterday. I know this is a difficult time for you and your family, and I just felt like we ought to do something more, so I've gone ahead and credited your account for half the cost."

"You what?"

"The shoes that were delayed will still arrive tomorrow, but I'm refunding half of your money."

"Wow! You're joking. That's amazing. Why would you do that?"

"Well, after hearing why you ordered them, it seemed to me like the last thing you needed was for this shoe order to add any more stress to your life, so I just wanted to apologize for the delay and make it right if we could. So you should see that credit back on your card within forty-eight hours."

"That's just . . . I don't know what to say. That's really generous of you. I told the woman on the phone yesterday that the memorial service had to be pushed back because of the weather. So the shoes coming late isn't even that big of a deal, so long as they get here."

"I understand, and I'm very glad they'll get there in time for the service. I'm just so sorry for your loss."

Susan paused. "Thank you. I appreciate that. We're all just so heartbroken . . ."

We're known for striving to deliver some of the best customer service in the business, and it's my job as a Customer Loyalty Team (CLT) lead to help make sure that continues. As such, I do spot checks of our customer service call logs to make sure that people who call in with a question or concern about something are being taken care of as they should be. I'm not sure why I happened to review that particular call that day—it truly was random—but I was immediately struck by what I heard.

> One interesting challenge we have is when we hire employees with prior call center experience. We sometimes have to untrain old bad habits and encourage new employees to focus more on WOWing the customer instead of minimizing call times and costs to the company if it's in service of a better customer experience. We have a team that audits random phone calls to look for coaching opportunities when we feel a rep provided good but not necessarily great service. One of my favorite quotes is from business author Jim Collins, who likes to say that good is the enemy of great.

Susan, this lovely woman with a Tennessee accent whom I was now on the phone with, had called in because most of her shoe order hadn't arrived as promised. Her order was unusual: eleven pairs of Lacoste sneakers, all of them red, in all different sizes. She told our phone rep that only *one* of those pairs of shoes had arrived, and that this was really important to her because these red shoes were going to be worn to a funeral—a memorial service for her teenage daughter's boyfriend, Luis.

The amazing thing is, Susan wasn't angry about the delay. She was just frustrated—you could hear it in her voice—and rightfully so. She wanted to make sure the shoes were still coming and would be there in time for this very important day. It turned out that Tennessee, which normally doesn't see much snow, had been hit by a major snowstorm, so a lot of planes and delivery services were shut down across the state. Our Customer Loyalty Team member explained that the shoes came from two different warehouses, and while one of the warehouses had been able to fulfill the shipment for one pair of shoes, all of the others that didn't arrive were coming from a different warehouse that was affected by the storms. Susan understood. Things happen. She said it would be all right, and the call ended cordially.

I wanted to follow up because I felt that our representative could have been more empathetic. She was friendly. She did some research and assured Susan that her shoes were now on their way. But she didn't offer much of an apology for the inconvenience and worry we had caused Susan and her family, and an apology certainly seemed warranted. I also thought that the shoes we had promised to deliver must've meant something really special to them. It wasn't a small order. It was $845 worth of shoes! There had to be some symbolism to ordering all of those particular red shoes to wear to a funeral, right? Clearly, we weren't just providing shoes to this family. We were providing something deeper, something that connected these people to this young man they'd lost.

> *Clearly, we weren't just providing shoes to this family. We were providing something deeper, something that connected these people to this young man they'd lost.*

That's why I called Susan and made the decision to give her half of her money back.

"I'll personally follow up in the morning to make sure those shoes arrive on time, okay? And if you have any issues with the sizes or anything, call me directly and I'll send a UPS truck to pick up the returns at your home and overnight the new sizes as needed at no additional charge."

"You'll do all of that?"

"Yes, it's my pleasure, Susan. And if I can help you with anything else, please don't hesitate to call. Let me give you my direct line, and my email address . . ."

I made sure Susan knew how to get in touch with me, and she thanked me again, and I thanked her for choosing Zappos, and that was that. But I couldn't stop thinking about Susan and her family. The moment I hung up the phone I ordered flowers to be shipped to her daughter the next day, along with a $100 gift certificate so she could buy herself something nice after all of this was over.

When I got home, I told my husband about the call. I kept talking about this woman and what she must be going through, and how awful it must be to see her daughter in pain, and I decided that I had come up a bit short on my phone call with her as well. I wanted to do something more, and I knew our company *would* do more. Susan and her daughter had called on Zappos to deliver in their time of need, and that is not something any company should take lightly.

As soon as I got to campus the next morning, I checked the computer, and I was happy to see that the shoes had been delivered. I glanced over at a picture of my dad on my desk, among a whole bunch of fun tchotchkes and little reminders that make my workspace so personal to me.

I picked up the phone.

"Hello?"

"Hi, Susan, it's Teri from Zappos again."

"Hi, Teri!"

"My computer is telling me that your shoes were delivered, but I just wanted to double-check that you got 'em."

"They're here! Thank you. And McKendree just received the beautiful roses you sent her, and that gift certificate. That was so incredibly thoughtful and generous, I don't know what to say."

"Well, I just wanted to do something a little extra. I didn't mention this to you yesterday, but I lost my father to cancer a few months ago. So I know how hard it can be."

"Oh no. I'm so sorry to hear that. I'm so sorry for your loss."

"Thank you. I appreciate that."

"But why the roses. How did you know?"

"Know what?" I asked.

"Luis used to send McKendree roses just like that when she was going through treatment."

"You're kidding."

"No. I don't know if you know this, but she and Luis met when they were in treatment."

"Oh my gosh."

"She's in remission now. She's doing great. But Luis used to send her roses just like that. Same color and everything. How did you know?"

"I didn't. I ordered a bouquet and the florist must've put it together. I'm not sure. Wow."

"Wow is right. I'm just so blown away by all of this. Thank you. And my daughter thanks you."

Susan began to cry, and I started to tear up, too.

"Hold on," she said, "let me put McKendree on the phone."

A few seconds later, I was on the phone with McKendree, who was just about the sweetest teenager I'd ever spoken to. She also started crying, and then I was crying even more. She told me I'd made her whole day.

When she put her mom back on the phone, Susan thanked me again and reiterated that she was sorry to hear about my father's passing.

"Thank you. He fought for a long, long time."

"Well, he certainly raised a good daughter."

That was when I paused. Her comment caught me off guard.

"I mean it," she continued. "If there was a little more of this sort of kindness and caring in the world, the world would be a much better place now, wouldn't it? Luis was that type of kind. He used to save toys all year long to take back to kids at the hospital in Honduras, where he was from, even while he was undergoing treatment. He would've loved to have seen McKendree's face when those flowers came to the door. He must be grinning ear to ear up in heaven right now. I just can't tell you what you've done for us today."

"Well, it's my pleasure," I said. "Look, I know you must be busy getting ready for tomorrow, so I don't want to keep you—"

"No, no, I'm a Southerner, and a mother. If there's one thing I don't mind doin' it's talkin'."

If there's one thing I've learned in this job it's that people, not just from the South, but people everywhere, like to talk. And they especially like to be *listened to*—even when the person doing the listening is a stranger on the phone who happens to work for an online retailer.

If there's one thing I've learned in this job it's that people everywhere like to talk. And they especially like to be listened to—even when the person doing the listening is a stranger on the phone.

"Well, okay, then. I do have a question for you, if you don't mind. I'm just so curious: Why the red shoes?"

Susan's voice soared as she told me the love story of McKendree and Luis, two teenagers who met at St. Jude Children's Hospital in Memphis in the fall of 2011 while undergoing treatment for cancer. It was like their own private version of *The Fault in Our Stars*, the way this joyful young man brought a smile to McKendree's face during the most trying time in her life, and the way Luis lit up at the joy and music McKendree brought to him. Together, they played guitar and sang to other kids on the second floor of the cancer ward at that hospital. They became best friends, and a fixture of happiness for other kids who were fighting for their lives, along with their families. Not to mention an inspiration to the doctors and nurses who worked so hard to save children every day.

Luis had already been fighting cancer for some time before McKendree came into his life. At one point, doctors were sure they were going to have to amputate his leg to stop the cancer. Luis was crushed. To lift his spirits, his parents scrimped and saved and managed to buy Luis a pair of red shoes that he coveted: a pair of red Lacoste sneakers that he'd spied in a shop window shortly after coming to America for his treatment. He wore them right up until the very last second before his scheduled surgery—and when he woke up in his hospital room after the surgery was completed, he looked down and saw both of his legs. The doctors didn't have to amputate after all.

From that day forward, Luis loved to wear those red shoes. In fact, his wish was to go hang-gliding in his favorite red Lacoste sneakers—a wish he accomplished while wearing the biggest smile anyone had ever seen.

The thing about cancer is it doesn't always show itself. Sometimes, what you see on the outside, the smile on someone's face, doesn't reveal what's happening under the skin. In early February 2015, Luis's health took a drastic turn for the worse. And with almost no warning at all, on Valentine's Day, of all days, he died.

McKendree was devastated. Everyone was devastated.

Susan cried when she told me. I cried, too.

That was when she told me it was McKendree's personal wish that she and all of their mutual friends who went through treatment together at St. Jude should wear red shoes to Luis's funeral. That was why Susan called Zappos and placed her multiple-red-shoe order. And now, here we were, on the phone with each other, in tears.

If that call had ended right there and I never spoke to Susan ever again, it would have gone down as one of the most memorable and touching interactions I'd ever had with a stranger in my whole life.

But it didn't end there. Not even close.

When good things happen here at Zappos, we share our stories with our coworkers. And no sooner did I share the story of Susan, McKendree, and Luis with a few other members of my Zappos family that the ideas started flying.

"Let's do something really special for McKendree. She must be so heartbroken."

"Maybe we could bring her and her family out here to Vegas."

"Yeah! A vacation."

"Maybe she could bring a few friends. Like, those friends from St. Jude who knew Luis. The ones who all wore the red shoes."

"Yes! And what if we threw them a party? A celebration of life. A celebration of Luis!"

Suddenly multiple departments within our company were collaborating on putting together a trip of a lifetime for McKendree and her friends and family. When all of the pieces were in place, we sent them a video saying, "Guess what? You're coming to Vegas!"

McKendree and her mom couldn't understand why we were being so nice and doing so much for them.

Our answer was—and always is—"Why not?" McKendree's story touched us, and we wanted to honor that. To honor her. To honor Luis. To honor Susan for everything she'd done to support her daughter. They all deserved some fun, didn't they? Plus, McKendree was graduating high school and still fighting her own battle with cancer. We thought she deserved a breather.

Why not?

"They made us feel like the most special people in the whole world," McKendree recalls of her trip to Vegas. (McKendree is in college now. She managed to get herself a full scholarship while undergoing treatment for cancer, so she's pretty inspiring all by herself!) "I'd never been to Vegas or anything close, and everything was thought out for us, every detail. We had so much fun. I don't think I'd smiled and laughed that much for as long as I can remember."

I'll never forget the moment McKendree and Susan came walking into the office and we met face-to-face for the very first time. I had watched a video of them that St. Jude had posted, so I already knew what they looked like. But what I wasn't prepared for was the flood of emotion. As I put my arms around these two people whom I had come to know on the phone, I started crying. It was such a moment for all three of us. A moment of pure joy. They started crying, too! I still tear up thinking about it.

My colleagues went all out for the party that night. We picked up McKendree and her friends in a limo, and we laid out a red carpet, and a large number of people from our staff stayed late just to set it all up and experience this celebration with them— including our CEO, Tony Hsieh. He found the whole thing so moving that he wound up sticking around all night. He was one of the last people to leave.

"The whole night was magic," McKendree says. "The people at Zappos put so much preparation into it, and they projected all of my favorite pictures of Luis and me together on one of the walls. They had a mariachi band, and some the staff did choreographed dances, and this amazing local singer played a bunch of music that was so special to Luis and me, including our favorite song, "Live Forever," by Drew Holcomb. A man named Miguel, who's one of the artists at Zappos, gave me two red shoes that he'd painted—one with Luis's face on it and the other with my face. I keep them in a shadow box in my room.

"It was just beyond anything I'd ever imagined happening to me in my whole life," McKendree continues. "When I look back on it I'm like, 'Did that really happen?' I've never had anyone make me feel that special besides Luis. I hadn't felt like that in a really long time. They somehow made me feel the way *he* would make me feel."

It was emotional for me, too—for all of us who were there. I don't think there was a dry eye in the house. Apparently Luis had a favorite saying that he used to quote all the time: "Where there is a pulse, there is a purpose." More than one person mentioned it at the microphone over the course of that night. And as we were reminded of that saying over and

> "Where there is a pulse, there is a purpose."

over again during the party, many of us in that room felt more inspired than ever to try to live up to our own personal purpose.

When McKendree's family got home to Tennessee, the celebration still wasn't over. Word of what happened spread everywhere. People started talking about it on social media. Someone started a hashtag using the phrase "Operation Red Shoes."

It was remarkable. What started out in sadness was evolving through this connection we'd made. By connecting and sharing our stories we were almost magically forming a whole new tribe of support for McKendree.

"Before long," Susan recalls, "we felt like we ought to do something for them in return, to show the folks at Zappos first-hand what Luis and what other patients at St. Jude experience. We thought it would be so much fun to turn the tables, to fly Teri and the folks who instigated the trip and the party out to Memphis. McKendree even talked about using her Make-a-Wish to fund that trip—but she didn't have to. Once the idea got back to St. Jude, some friends there stepped up and helped fund the trip themselves."

What can I say? The trip to Memphis was completely unexpected and completely amazing. We spent time at the hospital having a painting party with some of the kids. Susan and McKendree took us to Graceland and down to Beale Street. We felt so honored and so touched that this family and that hospital would reciprocate in that way.

Spending time together in Las Vegas and Tennessee led to something more: Susan and I had a chance to talk, *a lot*, and to this day Susan and I talk and text and email and keep in touch on a regular basis. We developed a friendship that I'm pretty sure will last the rest of our lives.

In the fall of 2015, McKendree, along with her sister, Bizzy, and Luis's friends Allie and Hailey, launched a nonprofit in Luis's memory: Operation Red Shoes (ORS). It's a charity designed specifically to help families with teens and kids with their needs as they go through cancer treatments. A bunch of people here at Zappos made personal donations to help get it started.

"We've got all kinds of support, including some celebrity supporters," Susan tells me. "David Mickey Evans, writer and director of *The Sandlot* (1993), gave ORS the first large donation. I really do think this is going to turn into a major nonprofit that will help with some of the unique situations teens who are battling this disease find themselves in. Our goal is that it will keep growing and continue doing good work in Luis's honor long after all of us are gone."

And that's still not all! Another sort of legacy project got started around the same time, too. Luis had a dog, a Siberian Husky named Luna, that he had left to McKendree.

"At first I didn't know what to do with her," she says. "Luna didn't even really like me. She was so protective of Luis that she used to wedge herself between the two of us on his couch! But she likes me now. We're friends. And we decided to breed her, to help spread even more of Luis's joy to others. Three of the puppies actually went into training to be service dogs for children with cancer."

One of the puppies wound up going to Tia Zuniga, a Zappos team member who helped make Operation Red Shoes happen. She brings that dog into the office now just to hang out with her team and brighten all of their days.

Like I said earlier: Opening your heart changes everything. And what Zappos has given to me and to all of us who work here is proof that business can have a heart, too. And when that heart is open, truly open, amazing things unfold.

Christa Foley
Head of Brand Vision, Head of Talent Acquisition, and Head of External Culture Training
Avid reader. No joke, I read four to five books per week.

In Greek mythology, Cerberus (or Kerberos), often called the Hound of Hades, is a three-headed dog that guards the gates of the Underworld to prevent the dead from leaving. I think of Christa as the three-headed gatekeeper of Zappos' culture and brand. She's not afraid to put her foot down anytime someone suggests doing something that may seem minor in the moment but might be the first step of a slippery slope that compromises our values in the long run.

The "Operation Red Shoes" story didn't happen by accident.

It didn't happen by chance, either.

It happened by design.

The possibility for great things to happen is simply built into the corporate structure here at Zappos—a direct reflection of our core values. And it's the kind of thing you can make happen at your company or small business, and in your life, too.

As Head of External Culture Training, I am lucky to lead an amazing team of Zapponians tasked with sharing the lessons (that is, "insights") we've learned here at Zappos with other business leaders across the country and around the world. So I couldn't be happier to see Operation Red Shoes kick off this employee-driven book, because it's such a great example of what can happen when everything we hope to accomplish at this company comes together.

> *Zappos Insights is the official name of the team that provides various training and coaching programs, including culture training ("Culture Camp"), customer service training ("School of WOW"), and external speaking ("Zappos Represents!").*

TONY

Many people think that Zappos is a website that sells shoes. But that's just what we are on the surface. What we *really* are, what we've always been, is a service company that just happens to sell shoes (and other products). We are truly a company built on putting service first. For us, it's all about establishing and nurturing personal human connections.

> *Internally, we have an acronym called PEC to describe what we are trying to accomplish with each and every customer interaction: Personal Emotional Connection.*

TONY

The depth of personal connection that Teri made on the phone with Susan and McKendree is something every one of us here at Zappos strives to make with every customer we encounter every day.

There's a lot of buzz in the business world today about creating a "customer-obsessed culture." The idea is that customers are *everything* to your business, and they need to be treated like the dollar-wielding, camera-phone-touting, social-media-driving powerhouses they are if any modern-day business wants to survive, let alone make a profit.

But at Zappos we don't look at it quite that way. Not that we don't have what some might call a customer-obsessed culture here. We do. We think about our customers *all the time*. But what do we mean when we talk about "customers"? And how do we interpret the concept of being "obsessed" with them?

There's no one formula to follow. At Zappos, customer service isn't about following a checklist or a script. It isn't about obsessively responding to customer Tweets in real time, or trying to act fast to quell customer complaints—although both of those things are important if done authentically and for the right reasons. It doesn't mean that we give things away for free all the time, or that we're putting on some sort of an act to try to get customers to like us, either. In fact, just the opposite is true.

The heart of Zappos' culture is that we view our customers as much more than a source of transactions. We strive to understand our customers' needs and to recognize that, in some cases, an order of shoes or some other product can mean much more. The real magic of our business culture is that we see our customers as humans. We see them as family. We see them as our neighbors and our friends. We see them as fellow employees. We see them . . . as *us*.

> Many people think that Zappos is a website that sells shoes. But that's just what we are on the surface. What we really are, what we've always been, is a service company that just happens to sell shoes.

And we know that the best thing we can do for each other is to treat each other authentically, the way humans should be treated under the best of circumstances. Which means that we do our best to lead with our hearts and to try to do the right thing for *all* of our customers, *all* of the time.

We want our customers to be happy. Truly happy. And we want to keep spreading that happiness around.

That's why our employees wanted to put this book together: We've been working on our service-first mentality for nearly twenty years. I've been here for most of those years, and I can tell you we didn't come to this conclusion overnight. It took time for us to understand that this mindset works best when it's genuine. What we do at work and what we do at home isn't and shouldn't be two different things, because putting service first matters as much in business as it does in life. It took us years to fully grasp just how possible it is for a business to act more human, to have a little more heart, and to learn that doing the *right* things instead of just the profitable things actually creates more "profit" for everyone. And we are still learning every day.

> At Zappos, our core values are an honest part of everything we do. They are guardrails that guide our way.

We've heard that we have done something pretty unique at Zappos: We've been able to retain our brand and our culture even after a major acquisition. A decade after being acquired by one of the biggest companies in the world—Amazon—we're still prioritizing our customers and our culture more than ever.

So how does a company grow from scratch into a business that's worthy of a $1.2 billion acquisition, and *then* survive and keep its core solid, all while continuing to grow in a rapidly changing environment? How can a company develop that type of resilience?

We believe that it all comes down to two pillars.

The first is a set of core values from which everything starts and ends. These aren't the type of "corporate values" or "mission statements" that get discussed in meetings and put on some document and forgotten. At Zappos, our core values are an honest part of everything we do. They are the guardrails that guide our way. Kind of like the Constitution, they serve as the basis of every decision we make and every venture we tackle. Our core values allow us to always know where we stand, so we can rest assured that we're always moving forward with our compass pointed in the right direction.

Our core values were discussed at length in Tony's first book, *Delivering Happiness*. But for those who've never seen them (and as a reminder for those who have), our core values at Zappos are:

1. Deliver WOW Through Service
2. Embrace and Drive Change
3. Create Fun and a Little Weirdness
4. Be Adventurous, Creative, and Open-Minded
5. Pursue Growth and Learning
6. Build Open and Honest Relationships with Communication
7. Build a Positive Team and Family Spirit
8. Do More with Less
9. Be Passionate and Determined
10. Be Humble

You'll see each of these core values in action over the course of this book. You can also take a deep dive into our Oath of Employment (see page 235). It's a document we give to all new hires, and beyond listing Zappos' Ten Core Values, it defines exactly what we mean by each one in detail. The oath is our signal to every employee that keeping true to our core values, our culture, is the right and responsibility of all of us.

Core values matter. When they're present, when they're solid, they sit at the foundation of every decision and every move you make. When they're not there? Well, we believe that's part of the reason some businesses might waver under pressure or struggle to make good decisions aligned with their brand and values.

The second pillar of our company? At Zappos, what we've found is that every ounce of our success depends on our employees. Hiring the right people and then trusting those people to have our company's—as well as our customers'—best interests at heart matters as much as anything else we could ever hope to design into the structure of our business.

After all, what is a company made of if not its people?

And putting people first is what service is all about.

PEOPLE POWER

Hollie Delaney
Chief Human Resources Officer
I trained dolphins after college.

I was fed up. I'd worked in HR for years, in a whole bunch of different environments, from a casino, to a water park, to e-commerce, and finally for brick-and-mortar retail, and, to be frank, I just didn't like what was I doing. I felt like all I did was enforce rules all day long, and deal with compliance issues, and tell people what they were doing wrong. There was nothing fun about it. Nothing uplifting.

I didn't even feel like I was *me* when I was at work. I didn't dress the way I like to dress. I'm a ripped jeans and t-shirt kind of woman, and at one of my prior HR jobs they made us wear stockings. Like, *pantyhose*. Every day. *Why?* Because that was the way it had always been done. Truly, there was no other reason.

When I was at work at my previous job, I didn't act like I normally act. It was like I put on a persona when I walked through the door. Work was just a job, and sometimes a *miserable* job, that I dragged myself to every morning only to watch the clock in the afternoon, just waiting to go home to my family and be me again.

> Zappos' HR department is like no other HR department I'd ever encountered. It's fun and a little bit weird, just like me.

When I hit the wall with my last job in retail, I made up my mind not only to leave but also to change careers. I was done with HR. All I needed was a temporary job to get me by while I figured out my next steps.

Of course, that was easier said than done. HR is what I was trained in. It's what filled up my résumé. So when I looked into employment at Zappos for what I truly believed would be a short stay, I grudgingly applied for an HR position. It wasn't the whole new world I was hoping for, but I had heard they were a fun company. I thought maybe it would at least be a somewhat enjoyable place to work while I figured out how to transition to an entirely different career.

I remember one of the first things the person who interviewed me asked was, "How would your current manager describe you?" And I replied, "They'd say I was fun, but a little weird."

"Really?" she said. "That's one of our core values: 'Create Fun and a Little Weirdness.'"

"Oh," I said, surprised and honestly a little skeptical. Zappos wasn't widely known back then. I hadn't heard a word about their "core values" or really much of anything else. (Turns out, they'd only just finalized the Core Values list that very year.)

"That's weird," I said out loud.

I wonder if Hollie laughed at her own joke on the inside.

TONY

It turned out that Zappos and I shared a lot of core values, once I learned what those were. I got hired. I stuck around. I moved up the ladder to become head of HR, and, more than twelve years later, I'm still here. The job wasn't so temporary after all!

You see, I quickly discovered that Zappos' HR department is like no other HR department I'd ever encountered. It's fun and a little bit weird, just like me. And it's built on actually putting the "human" in human resources.

When you hire people who are aligned with your values and the company's values, things just click—for the employee *and* for the company.

So how do we figure out who to hire?

First off, take our time. After all, if our employees are our greatest resource, it only makes sense that we would put some serious effort into finding the right humans for our company. The minute our recruiters start talking to candidates, from the first phone call or email through several rounds xxof interviews, they bring up the Core Values and ask behavioral-based questions to see if the candidates understand and align with those values. We dig right in to great customer service, and talk about understanding change, and being humble, and taking chances, taking risks, and being ready to learn. Our hiring process is not just about the résumés. It's about finding out who these candidates are as human beings.

When we get to a final decision phase, the candidates spend the day—sometimes multiple days—on site, getting to know the whole company. They're given tours of the campus so they can see our values in action. They join us for lunches and after-work happy hours, just so we can see how they interact with other employees.

Once they're hired, we put them through an extensive new-hire training (NHT) and onboarding process. We're not talking one or two days. Our onboarding is four *weeks*! Four weeks in which our new Zapponians get a deep dive into our history, our core values, and who we are as a company. And that onboarding is really an extension of the hiring process. If we decide at the end of those four weeks that they're just not a good fit with one or more of our core values, we let candidates know we're going to let them go; and if they themselves don't feel that they're a good fit for Zappos, we want them to be comfortable walking away as well. We truly want our potential employees to ask themselves, "Is this really what I want? Did I sign up for the right thing? Is working at Zappos really going to make me happy?" And we want them to ask these questions *before* they're entrenched, *before* they wind up working for six or eight or ten months or a year in a place they really don't like, only to quit and put us back at square one with refilling the position.

How do we get our new recruits to put up with all of that?

We give them an offer to quit at the end of training and if they choose to take that offer, they receive a month's pay. Is that a costly process? Yes and no. A small percentage of new hires does elect to quit. And we've found that it's actually cost effective, because we're not just hiring people. We're hiring the *right* people. People who have a service-first mindset. People who want to be here because we fit them, too, and who, in most cases, are going to stick around for the long haul—the way I did—and hopefully make our company better for the hard work we all put in early on.

Christa Foley
Head of Brand Vision, Head of Talent Acquisition, and Head of External Culture Training
I was late to the party with Game of Thrones, *but I* love *it.*

*Over the years we've developed a long list of ques-*tions around each of our core values, and they help us determine whether someone is going to align with our core values and fit our culture, or not. I mean, someone who's very rigid, who can't adapt to change, who wants to live by the standard old corporate rules—they're definitely not going to fit in here, right? It's important to catch those sorts of red flags early on. And we've found that a lot can be gained by asking sort of off-the-wall questions, like "How lucky do you feel you are?" or "If every time you walked into a room a theme song played, what would that be, and why?" These quirky questions can lead to some serious conversations and shine a light on somebody's values.

We also decided a long time ago that culture fit *always* trumps a technical fit when hiring. Just because someone is great at their particular job at this particular moment doesn't mean they're going to be a good fit down the line when systems change, or practices change, or the marketplace changes, or we move to a new location, or whatever it is they might have to adapt to. If

"Embracing and Driving Change" isn't something they value, they wouldn't enjoy working at Zappos—and they wouldn't be very successful here.

Mostly, though, we want to make sure our new hires understand what we mean by customer service. That a "customer" is any person they come in contact with, including coworkers. Just because a person can interface with a computer doesn't mean they're on board with "Delivering WOW Through Service" to their fellow human beings in the office, or elsewhere. It's important that we see who they are, as an authentic person, to know if their core values align with ours.

Maritza Lewis
Engage Team
My parents have five daughters, but they decided to name their restaurant after me. I guess I'm the favorite. :P

*"Culture" is not about conforming here. We value diver-*sity. We value individuality and personal growth. It's the reason I've stayed and taken on different roles here over the last twelve or thirteen years—just like Hollie and so many people who've stuck around—because Zappos values me as a whole person and *wants* me to flourish.

We don't expect everyone to be the same. Not at all! But the most important thing about building a workforce and hiring the right people is figuring out: How are these people going to work together, and work together extremely well, to deliver great service and to make your company grow?

MEGAN
I hate wearing shoes when I'm teaching.

VERONICA
I believe all life lessons can be learned from watching My Little Pony: Friendship Is Magic.

STEPHANIE
I love boxing and trying to coerce people into coming to boxing class with me.

Megan Petrini, Veronica Montanez, and Stephanie Hudec
Onboarding

 VERONICA The reason we have ridiculously high expectations during new-hire training and onboarding is because our company culture actually comes down to one thing: Relationships. Our company isn't siloed. We work really, really hard to make sure that we're not isolated from each other as we continue to grow. So everyone needs to have the same foundation. You need to be here every day. You need to show us that you have good time management. You have to pass a final, just like everybody else. You have to pass a quality check, just like everybody else. You have to

> *Our company culture actually comes down to one thing: Relationships. Our company isn't siloed. We work really, really hard to make sure that we're not isolated from each other as we continue to grow.*

get on the phones, regardless of the position you're being hired into, to show us that you're the right fit for the company, not just one department.

Even though the re-cruitment process is long and the vetting is thorough, our new-hire training is basically the last stop. Because during a month of training, you're going to see a person's true colors come out. You're going to find out if they're someone who abuses an attendance policy, or who tries to skirt around the edges of an assignment, or who doesn't actually work well with a team.

It's funny because around week two, a lot of the trainees are like, "We're gonna die here!" It feels really long. But by week four, people are like, "I can't believe we're graduating on Friday!" Assuming they're actually a good fit, they'll have built great relationships and made friends, and are actually now living embodiments of the foundation of our culture. And if they're not a good fit, well, then we pay them to leave. And that's a pretty great deal for all involved.

MEGAN The foundation winds up being "You're a part of the team." We do a lot of team building, like a middle school–style egg drop, where you work with a team to make a contraption to hold and protect an egg, and then we drop the eggs from the second story of the building and see which eggs go unbroken. These activities seem like fun and games at first, but they're not *just* fun. We learn our core values through doing. So "Do More with Less," all of the team and family spirit we talk about, it all comes into play.

STEPHANIE A lot of the team-building activities are timed, so there's no time to think about what might go wrong. That pushes another thing we love here at Zappos: "Don't think about how it's not going to work. Imagine it done, imagine it working, and work backward from there." We want them to get in the habit of trying new things, fearlessly, and building on top of each other's ideas and learning from each other's failures.

VERONICA At the end of training, there's an office parade, people dressing up in costumes and going through campus—it's all about having fun and letting people know that it's okay to be themselves here. When we put people on the phones we want them to be themselves, which is what helps them relate to our customers authentically. You can be on the phones or be the CFO of the company—no matter what your role is, we want you to provide the Zappos experience 100 percent of the time. You're going to do that in your own unique way. There's no one way to do it. But by providing the foundation of training, we know that you'll be able to go out there and represent the company in every interaction just by being your real self.

MEGAN That's actually the last conversation we have with new hires, right after they graduate. We pull them back into the classroom and remind them, "You've had this full immersion into the Zappos culture, to really understand what it's all about. But now, you have to be the one to continue this. No one else can force it to happen. You just have to go out there and make sure that you continue this."

Our job is done when they have the right tools to go out and do it themselves.

VERONICA It's amazing to see people relax, too. Some of them will come in from a corporate background and show up on the first day in a dress shirt and slacks, thinking it's a casual look. And by the end of NHT, they're in their favorite band t-shirt. It's a metamorphosis. And it's about way more than how they dress. The metamorphosis unlocks their creativity and excitement. They come to realize that their individuality is actually valued here. That it matters to Zappos that they bring their own unique stuff to the table that no one else can bring.

MEGAN Truly, one thing no one could ever accuse us of is judging a book by its cover.

TONY

Why would we? We want our whole company to work, and for that, we need to look at each individual we're hiring. Not just the suit they wear or the résumé they bring, but the whole person. We want to value the whole person we're bringing into our family.

Johnnie Brockett
Treasury and Accounts Receivable
I used to be terrible at math. Now I work in Treasury.

I'll say right up front that I recognize that a lot of companies wouldn't even think about hiring me just because of the way I look. I've got tattoos and gold teeth. I don't look like a typical "corporate employee."

I grew up in Fayetteville, North Carolina, where the Army's Fort Bragg is located. It's a tough town, man. I fit right in there. But walking into HR in most companies, I could tell they closed the door to hiring me before I even said my name.

Zappos was a different story. They care about what your *mind* can do, and how much you care about other people, and whether you value doing the right thing, the *honest* thing—'cause all of that is a whole lot more important than how a person looks on the outside.

Looks can be deceiving.

Case in point: About two weeks after I started, we were still in class, and we got invited to a meeting at Downtown Cocktail Room. We were sitting at this big table, and everybody's got on Chuck Taylors and Zappos t-shirts, and little did I know I was sitting there with some team leads, managers, and executives—*everybody*. And we were just hanging out! That's how this company is.

It's amazing how much trust they've put in me over the years, too. I've grown here into something that I never imagined for myself. I went to college for zero years. Zero! All of my education on the business side has been right here at work. I've moved up. I've moved into positions where I was needed. And just last week I was handling a quarter of a billion dollars in transactions. Just me. No one else.

Bhawna Provenzano
Head of Benefits and Wellness
I have traveled to over fifteen countries and can't wait for our next adventure!

We hire employees who care, who want to make a difference, and we see it as our job to provide benefits that make a difference to our employees and show them that we care, too.

First of all, we want to remove as many barriers as possible for our employees. We want to make sure they're covered in case there are catastrophic events. We want to make sure that their medical care and the costs that are associated with it won't ever throw them into bankruptcy. But that's just a start. We want our employees to feel safe. To feel healthy. To feel covered, so they don't have to worry every day about basic things. We make the conscientious decision to say, "Okay, we are going to pay more and spend more on benefits, and to do it purposefully. Mindfully." And like any other company, we have to be mindful of costs, right? But that's not the number one thing for us.

Our employees are number one.

Our employees, in addition to our core values and culture, are our north star.

Why would we not want to WOW them?

So in addition to offering the best-possible health care plans, with expansive maternity and paternity leave and, honestly, the sort of support that so many people dream about at other companies, we offer all sorts of on-site benefits and perks as well. For example, the company pays for pet adoptions. We'll bring a bunch of little doggies on site and let employees play with them as a fun, relaxing thing to do, and if anyone really bonds with and wants to take one of the dogs home as a pet, we'll cover the adoption fee. That may seem frivolous in the corporate world, but the idea came from an employee, and people love it!

Close to 90 percent of our benefit ideas and wellness ideas come from employee feedback. They'll email us and be like, "What do you think about this? What about that?" And oftentimes we'll try new ideas simply because we can—simply because we want to offer the best possible service to our employees.

We'll pay the entry fees for employees who want to run marathons or 5Ks for a cause.

There are fitness classes here during work hours. Employees can purchase meal prep plans for themselves and for their families. We have an outdoor space where people can partake in community gardening.

Maritza Lewis
Engage Team

My husband and I met at work before we both came to Zappos, but we didn't dare date at our previous job. It was forbidden. Here? There are lots of couples. Dating coworkers isn't discouraged. I mean, people understand not to take it to the extreme and, like, make out in front of your coworkers and stuff, but there aren't any rules about it. We're all adults. Since Zappos is really careful during the hiring process to find people who just sort of "get it," who fit the culture, who want to do right by the people around them, it just works.

One of my roles here is to teach eight hours of company history during new-hire training, and I even talk about this dating business as part of our company history. Our founder, Nick Swinmurn, met his wife, Gabby, here. When Nick started dating Gabby, one of our HR representatives at the time pulled him into a room and said, "Nick, what the hell are you doing? You're the founder of this company. You can't date your employees!" And he was like, "What?"

The HR rep said, "This could end great and you end up marrying her, or—*or*—this could end really badly and she'll take everything you have!" And Nick looked at her and said that he would much rather assume that something positive would happen than to focus on the worst possible outcome.

Nick and Gabby *did* marry, in fact, and they have a son. Today, there are lots of other couples here at Zappos who work side by side in some cases, and in different departments in others. The only policy we have is that you can't date someone you report to, or vice versa.

When you hire employees you trust, who fit your company culture, then you can trust them to do the right thing.

I think one of the most unique things I've found about working here at Zappos is that 20 percent of your time is really meant to build relationships and bond with your coworkers and colleagues from other teams all across the company. You don't find that in a lot of organizations, because, in most organizations, if you're not sitting at your desk, well, guess what? You're going to get in trouble. But here, the site is built in such a way that the entire campus is Wi-Fi friendly. You have little places to work all over. It's been drilled into us that it's okay for you *not* to sit at your desk. Actually, we would *rather* you not sit at your desk.

You can get your nails done, or you can paint pottery, or get your oil changed or get a car wash while your car's just sitting in the parking garage all day, rather than spending time doing those things after work or on the weekend. Having a gym on site matters to a lot of employees. We have showers here so you can go during work. And the fitness classes—even they contribute to team building. There are whole teams that go together and have fun with yoga classes and dance classes in the middle of the workday.

It all goes back to removing barriers for the employee. We're thinking holistically when we're providing these things. It's about service. It's about "What can we do to make the employees' lives better?"

That includes paying for as much coverage and as many benefits as possible for our employees' families as well—because if someone is worried about the health of their spouse or their child, that's going to affect their ability to concentrate at work, and ultimately to deliver great service to our customers, and to serve our business interests. When the Affordable Care Act (ACA) came along, we were already doing most of the parts of it related to families, which meant there was little to no adjustment for us to make to comply with the new law. We were already doing those things because they were the right things to do. I heard about some real struggles that went on at other companies. There was a huge cost involved trying to come into compliance—a loss of productivity, lots of confusion. For us, it was easy. Which just goes to show that caring about our employees and doing the right thing for them isn't difficult. It's not burdensome. It's actually easier and more cost-efficient in the long run!

Life doesn't end when you come to work, and the feeling of working for the Zappos family, which we talk about here a lot, should not end when you go home.

I don't think it's a coincidence that Google and Facebook and some of the most profitable, fastest-growing companies in the country have cute offices and strong benefits plans. But such companies are still few and far between. With Zappos, it's "work hard, play hard." I mean, the toys in the office, the nap rooms, the fun events we hold every week, the bar we built right on campus—the fringe benefits are what get highlighted in magazine articles, but people don't look much at the other side of it, which is the incredibly hard work that people do here to maintain and grow this company every day.

> *The instigator and creator of the bar in our lobby is Letha Myles, who is one of our tour guides but also moonlights as a bartender around downtown Vegas. She also happens to love Prince (or the artist formerly known as Prince) more than life itself. (Pretty Woman fans: see what I did there? ☺) Anyway, Letha came up with the perfect name for the bar: 1999. (Zappos was founded in 1999 for those of you paying attention.)*

—TONY

We wouldn't be where we are after our first twenty years without a lot of incredibly hard work, and I just don't think that anyone would work quite so hard if it weren't for the feeling of true support that this company offers. It goes both ways.

Little things aren't frivolous. The fact is, if somebody can come wash your car and give it an oil change while you're here at work, you can then spend that hour or two on the weekend with your family, so you can truly focus on living life when you're at home and not waste an entire weekend running errands. Then you can come back to work on Monday morning and *not* feel like you missed your chance to be with your family because you were stuck in an office all day and not allowed to leave your desk. It's just a different way of looking at things. And the benefits of that to the company, and to our customers—it's enormous compared to the nominal cost associated with some of these things.

Do right by your employees and they'll do right by you.

If our employees are truly our most important resource, then it simply makes sense to treat them accordingly. We want them to feel WOWed by our company culture, the same way we want our paying customers to feel WOWed by it, too. So we do as much as we possibly can.

It just seems like common sense, doesn't it? Do right by your employees and they'll do right by you.

INDIVIDUALITY WELCOMED

Jeff Lewis
Customer Service Technology

I once received a call from a customer asking about our "Joke of the Day." He explained that he was a janitorial supervisor at the McMurdo Research Station—in Antarctica, of all places—and that every Monday, his team would call in to our main line during their weekly meeting to listen to our Joke of the Day. He said that our jokes were the highlight of the meeting for his staff, and that they wanted to know if they might be able to contribute some jokes. We took them up on it, and a week later we started playing the jokes they had sent over.

Roughly a month after this interaction, we received a large box full of candy from the McMurdo janitorial staff, filled with all kinds of candy from around the world. It took so long to get here from Antarctica that some of the candy was expired by the time it arrived, but the goodwill shown by the McMurdo team has always stuck with me.

Loren Becker
Community Team
I have webbed feet.

It was one of our employees who came up with the idea to offer a "Joke of the Day" option on our customer service line, and it's been going on for years now: Anyone who calls in can opt to be taken to the "Joke of the Day" before getting connected to CLT, if they so choose.

> *Um, Loren . . . I think it was, um, my idea, derived from my childhood shenanigan history of calling 976-JOKE without realizing the calls were not free. In my book* Delivering Happiness, *I wrote:*
>
> > *I asked if anyone had heard of 976 numbers. I had seen all sorts of ads on TV for different 976 numbers. You could call 976-JOKE, for example, to hear the joke of the day, at the cost of 99 cents a call. So we tried calling 976-JOKE, and heard a joke that wasn't very funny. We tried calling the number again to try to get a better joke, and all they did was replay the same one. In retrospect, I guess it made sense since it was supposed to be the joke of the day, not the joke of the minute.*

TONY

It wasn't a marketing idea. It wasn't designed to make calls shorter to keep our 800-number budget down (obviously, since it makes calls longer). It doesn't result in increased purchases, at least not directly. It was just something fun to do. A way to let customers know that we're a unique, fun place to call in to, and maybe even a way to relieve some tension if whoever's calling is having a bad day—which might include the fact that something was wrong with their order and they're now spending their valuable time calling customer service at Zappos.

The thing is, we're quirky here, and we want you to know it.

Our employees have the freedom to tell jokes, to send cards, to send gifts, to talk to callers or vendors or contractors for hours and hours if they strike up a good conversation. They have the freedom to be themselves. And freedom is a pretty rare thing in the workplace, isn't it?

When people come to tour our Downtown Las Vegas campus

which also happens to be the former Las Vegas City Hall

—and they do come, in the thousands, it's crazy!—they're excited by what they see. Like, the bar we built right next to the lobby, or employees playing video games and Skee-Ball in the company arcade in the middle of the day. They see employees stopping by the convenience store in our lobby, picking up some random item they forgot at home and need now, and they wish they could do that at their own places of work.

The freedom and autonomy we give to our employees isn't frivolous. It's purposeful. We want everyone here to know that they are allowed to use their best judgment, to do things on their own without asking permission. That they can take a risk and try new ideas without feeling like, "Oh, if I take this risk and it doesn't work out, I could get fired."

If we were a brand-new start-up, I think you could write off our quirky ways and dismiss them as something that wouldn't work anywhere else, and our critics certainly did that in our early days. But we've been around long enough now to have a meaningful track record, and I think more and more people are taking a look at this level of freedom we offer our staff and thinking, "Huh. Maybe there's something to all of that."

The freedom of expression and overall autonomy that's such a part of our culture isn't just important in the workplace. It's important to how we provide service to our customers. We know for a fact (because we've occasionally tried regulating things in ways that weren't "us") that if we get too uptight or too stuffy or too regulated, then our Customer Loyalty Team, the people on the phones—the front line that shares experiences with our customers—won't provide the same energy. If they're unhappy, if they're feeling stuffy, then they come off as unhappy and stuffy on the phone. On the other hand, if they've just come back from our company-wide Taco Tuesday, they're like, "Oh my gosh, thanks for calling. How was *your* day?" The energy you get from the office is translated to the customer. It all comes full circle.

The freedom and autonomy we give to our employees isn't frivolous. It's purposeful. We want everyone here to know that they are allowed to use their best judgment, to do things on their own without asking permission.

That's not to say that we don't have any rules here. We have guidelines. I mean, you don't let cars drive on the left side of the road, right? There are speed limits. There are definitely guidelines in life that help everyone enjoy their freedom without getting run off the road and wrecking each other's cars. And those guidelines change and shift and adapt over time, for sure. When I started on the phones fourteen years ago, there was a slight bit more freedom to give stuff away, or the feeling of, "Man, if they have the slightest issue, let's comp those shoes!" Our volume is so big now, we've had to pull back slightly on that one particular freedom we give to our CLT workers. But the last time I was back on the phones for a couple of hours, I gave a lady a pair of shoes during one conversation because it was the right thing to do. It's just that not every customer service call warrants that big of a response. A coupon or a simple replacement-exchange, or even just some kindness and understanding, goes a long way. But I can't think of a single time or a single way in which we've pulled back our employees' freedom to make choices and "do the right thing" themselves in any major way, in all these years.

As long as we stick to our core values and keep service first in everything we do, everything works out. Truly. Everything. Even if something goes wrong in the short term, in the long run? This formula works, and it works really well.

Kelly Smith
Experimental Marketing and Brand Strategy
I once got to hold a human brain! It was one of the strangest and coolest experiences I've ever had.

I like to think of responsibility as "response-ability"—the ability to respond. We give each of our employees true decision-making power, allowing them to lead with their hearts and show empathy by engaging with customers as trusted representatives of our company. There truly is no script. When it comes to making the right decision, we encourage our employees to go with their gut and to always "do the right thing," without having to ask a manager or go through some committee before they do it. On the phones, that means giving customers free or reduced-price merchandise to make up for unforeseen errors, or sometimes just to put smiles on their faces. It could mean sending cards or flowers to customers who need a pick-me-up. We budget for all of that because we know it's important. Not just because it feels good and makes our customers feel good, but because it's good for the business.

A little empathy goes a long way, and our customer loyalty numbers bear that out. We track comments across all sorts of social media to measure Zappos promotors versus detractors online, and while our industry usually gets around 60 percent positive responses, we routinely score around *90 percent positive*. We have an A+ rating with the Better Business Bureau, too. And in our own internal surveys, we routinely find that more than 98 percent of customers "feel that the Zappos family member you interacted with genuinely cares about you and your reason for contacting us."

Genuinely! We look for employees who genuinely care, who want to make the world a better place—and providing positive customer experiences actually does make the world a better place.

Somewhere along the line, customer service departments developed a bad reputation. In my opinion, far too many companies made the poor decision to chase short-term profits instead of the long-term gains of treating customers the way they themselves would want to be treated. And the result is that people all across America are ready for a fight every time they have to pick up a phone and ask for help, even when they paid good money for something and the company on the other end of the line is clearly at fault for not delivering what was promised. (Is there anyone who hasn't had a lousy customer service experience with the cable company, or an airline, or some other big industry we depend on to deliver services we need to function at home and at work?)

A lousy customer service call can ruin your whole day. We all know that.

Lauren Pappert
Customer Loyalty Team

I once got a call from a customer who mentioned he was a comedian performing in Washington, DC. Before jumping into the order, I asked him, "Are you funny?" I was trying to be the lovable heckler-type but I don't think my delivery was on point. He laughed it off and said he hoped he was funny because he was going onstage soon. As he placed his order, I soon realized he was a famous comedian who has starred in many of my favorite movies. *Awkward!* Turned out he couldn't get an order delivered to the hotel in time for his Saturday show, so he wanted to cancel the order. In true Zappos fashion, I let him know we would find a way to get them there. We searched high and low and found the exact same shoe available on Amazon with Saturday delivery. He was ecstatic and placed the order online before we even hung up! Zappos may not have delivered his shoes, but we delivered a lighthearted conversation, a solution focused around his needs, and happiness.

I'm hoping he put on a really good show that night and made a whole lot of people smile—and I love imagining that maybe our exchange played a tiny role in that.

But a great customer service call? With someone who genuinely cares and who's empowered to take care of you the way you ought to be taken care of? That can make your whole day better. And people who are treated right usually let their family and friends know about it. They come back as repeat customers, in a big way. (That's not conjecture. We've measured it. In the next chapter, our COO will explain just how big that return on investment is.) And they often find themselves paying it forward.

No joke: Kindness is contagious!

Check out these stories (in the blue boxes) from actual calls with Zappos customers to get a sense of what I mean.

Hollie Delaney
Chief Human Resources Officer
I'm a huge Vegas Golden Knights hockey fan! I go to all the home games and lots of the away games.

It all goes back to trust. At Zappos, we manage the 95 percent of people who are going to do things right. In other companies, HR is all about managing the 5 percent who are going to do things wrong, and making sure you're covered for that 5 percent, which means you're automatically assuming that basically everyone is going to do things wrong.

It's a totally different approach here. We actually trust that people are going to do the right thing. We start out assuming positive intent, which means we don't have to put many rules and policies in place at all. And guess what? I don't see any more issues or any more complaints here than I did in a company with all sorts of traditional rules in place. I've done the metrics to compare, like "How many complaints have I gotten?" or "How

Jeff Espersen
Head of Merchandising

One time during the holidays, this lady called in screaming at me because her packages were stolen. I had to hold the phone out at arm's length until she gave me a moment to speak. This lady was ready for a fight, and I think if I were working at some other company I might have cut her off and started questioning her: "Do you have any proof they were stolen? How do I know this isn't fraud and you just want more boots?" (She was saying that three pairs of boots had been stolen from the spot where the delivery service had left them.)

But this is Zappos. Our company trusts us to do the right thing, and we in turn trust that our customers aren't trying to rip us off, either. So I said, "Okay, I'm so sorry to hear they were stolen. Do you have the order information at all? Do you know what was on there? Let's see if we have those in stock." I just took care of her and sent her new stuff for free. She did not expect that. Toward the end of the call she said, "Wow, that was . . . that was *easy*."

She was so happy to know that the replacements for her stolen boots were on the way, it made up for every bit of anger she was feeling. And I have no doubt she told everyone she knows that story. And I bet she still tells that story whenever she wears those boots.

What did that cost us? Not much in the big scheme of things. But that good will goes a long way. Even *I* felt better after that call, like I'd done something nice and made someone's day a whole lot better.

> *We trust that people are going to do the right thing. We start out assuming positive intent, which means we don't have to put many rules and policies in place at all.*

many issues did I have in the old world of HR versus how many issues have I had here?" And there are actually fewer issues here than when we had all of the policies and procedures in place in my old jobs.

So instead of spending 95 percent of my time catering to compliance issues in order to deal with the five-percenters, I spend almost all of my time here working on the more important thing, which is how to make this company be a place where employees *want* to work.

TRUST IN ACTION

Tyler Williams
Head of Brand Aura
My favorite snack is Tim's Cascade jalapeño chips.

I've been here for about eight years now. Longest job I ever had. And one of my favorite stories happened when I was on Holiday Helper duty. That's when every employee at Zappos works the phones during the holiday season, just to alleviate some of the pressure on the Customer Loyalty Team. And I do mean every employee, going all the way to the top. It's awesome, because it keeps us all in touch and grounded. And when you're a Holiday Helper, you're kind of getting back into the swing of learning how to do the phones again. If you haven't done it for a while, you're a little nervous, and you're like, "I don't want to screw things up for somebody."

One time this elderly lady called in to return a pair of shoes, and she was really selling it, like, "My bunions hurt and I really tried to make these ones work, and I walked around the house . . ." My first instinct was to say, "Yeah, no problem. Go ahead and return them." But when I pulled up her account on the computer there were all sorts of alerts and notes from my colleagues. It turned out this woman had bought more than 100 pairs of shoes and returned every single one of them.

I went through the notes while she kept talking to me and making her case, and I realized there had been an ongoing argument between CLT reps over this woman for quite some time. Some of my colleagues felt protective, as if she were ripping us off by taking advantage of our free return policy. They were like, "We need to cut this lady off!" But other colleagues were saying, "Well, we've talked to her and she lives by herself. She has no family, she's on Social Security, and she's at a home. And having something come in the mail to her, even though she can't afford to keep it, brings her happiness." Finally I got to a note—and it was written by Tony, our CEO, who works the phones just like the rest of us during the holidays. And his note read, "Let her keep ordering the shoes. It makes her happy."

The bottom line is we trust our customers.

I was like, "WOW!"

That's the type of stuff that makes me fall in love with the company all over again. When I see things like that happen, I'm reminded that it's *real*. Everything we talk about here, all of our values: They're real. It's not like we're just putting on this "Delivering Happiness" thing like a show or a stunt or something.

The bottom line is we trust our customers. We trust that the vast majority of people in the world aren't out to hurt anybody. If a customer is returning lots of shoes, there's probably a good reason they're doing what they're doing. Do we lose some money on shipping to this one lady? Yeah. But it's not going to bankrupt us. We're delivering happiness. We're making her world a little brighter. There's value in that.

And sure, there are exceptions to the rule. There are scam artists. There are people trying to see what they can get away with. But this company has been at the front lines of customer service for twenty years now, and, statistically speaking, the number of con artists and thieves we encounter on a daily basis is zero. It's such a small percentage that we don't bother worrying about them. I mean, we don't ignore them. We don't let them get away with it. We do cut people off. We red-flag customers who've done wrong by us. We're not fools. But we don't treat all of our customers like crooks because of those very, very few who are.

I think that's a direct reflection of how the company treats us as employees, too. Once you make it through new-hire training, you're empowered here at Zappos. It's a really hard adjustment for some people to realize that there isn't some manager hovering over them, micromanaging their every move. Once you've been trained, once you're on the same page and a part of the team here, you're free to do whatever it takes to keep customers happy.

Most of our customers are happy to begin with. Serving them well is built into the ethos here, so most customers have nothing to complain about. Negative customer reviews and viral blasts on social media can make even a good company look bad real quick. But we flipped that coin on its head long before social media even got popular, by taking those rare dissatisfied customers and WOWing them—showing them such great service that they almost can't help but to tell all of their friends what an awesome experience they had at Zappos.

Working the phones here, you feel almost like you're the CEO of the company or something. It's just driven into you that there's almost nothing you *can't* do to make sure the customer is WOWed. It's just the polar opposite of what happens at most call centers, which I think is why "customer service" gets such a bad rap. When you call some customer service lines, it's almost as if they've been given a script to read and a protocol to follow that's specifically designed to annoy you and make you never want to do business with that company ever again. We've all had that experience. It's just so frustrating. But at Zappos, we're given the freedom to actually talk to customers. To ask them about their lives. To tell them jokes. To laugh with them. To cry with them. To listen to them, almost like we're their therapist for the day or something.

From the moment we come on board we're given the freedom to do what's right to make our customers happy. We have budgets set aside to send cards and flowers. We have a number of individuals who are passionate about sending out rewards and incentives to our best customers, too—so it's not just the squeaky wheels who get the grease, you know what I mean?

It costs the company money, sure, but we view that as brand investment. For less than the price of one Super Bowl ad (which we would never buy), we can service thousands of customers in the best way possible. And the word-of-mouth and social-media love that generates far outweighs the cost, every time.

Arun Rajan
Chief Operating Officer
I had to go to the ER at my first 8,000m Endurance Challenge—I learned that hydration is key for major endurance events. ☺

Mistakes happen: shipping failures, warehouse mix-ups, items going out to customers that are the wrong size or the wrong color. If you're dealing with any sizable sales volume, especially involving shipping, mistakes are inevitable. You can work to make the system as perfect as possible, and we've worked hard to keep improving the system and eliminating errors for two decades now. Still, things happen. And those mistakes generally make customers upset. But where I think many companies lose a tremendous opportunity is not doing everything they can to turn those mistakes into opportunities and those disgruntled customers into your best customers of all.

Let me give you an example of the extremes we'll go to in order to make sure customers are happy. In December 2017, we decided to boast a little bit about our shipping abilities just before Christmas. With a little over two days to go, we launched a major marketing campaign to let every one of our customers know: "If you order by noon on December 23rd, you're going to get your package in time for Christmas!"

Within an hour or so after that note went out to our email list, reaching tens of millions of customers, we received an email from our Fulfillment Center telling us that they had already reached capacity. They wouldn't be able to deliver a single package more until after December 25.

Panic set in.

We knew how many orders were pouring in, and we now faced the grim reality that a lot of customers were not going to get their packages by Christmas as promised.

We called an emergency meeting. A whole bunch of us gathered in a conference room and thought through the process. Could we hire more fulfillment staff? Rent our own delivery trucks? Send staff from Vegas to go deliver packages by hand? Some pretty wild ideas were tossed around until Tony said, "Just give it away."

So that's what we did: Anyone who ordered products from us that weren't delivered as promised received a full refund for the purchase.

Done.

We're talking somewhere between 10,000 and 15,000 orders. We sell some pretty pricey products on our site. Add shipping costs, and you can do the math. The financial teams at many companies would've said, "No way! There's no possible way we can take that hit."

But at Zappos, we didn't see it as a hit.

We saw it as a brand investment in Zappos itself.

It was the right thing to do.

Service is our brand, and our customers are everything. There was no way we were going to let our customers down en masse like that. Our DNA doesn't stomach a story of "Zappos let me down for Christmas."

Spending money on customers is an investment, and we invest everything we can into our customers. Just look at the Customer Loyalty Team. Of the 1,500 or so employees at Zappos, approximately 600 of them work directly in customer service. Exceptional service is the promise we make to our customers, so we invest whatever it takes in it.

When something goes wrong, we do everything we can to take care of our customers and to make it right. And here's the amazing part: We're more likely to retain them than customers who never experienced any problems with our service at all. For example, we followed the customers who were affected during Christmas 2017, those whose orders were negatively impacted and then salvaged, or whom we at least attempted to take care of by refunding their money. We found that, compared to our usual customers, these folks came back and purchased *more* from our site than they might have if nothing had gone wrong.

They're not the only ones. It's a pattern. We've been tracking this for some time now, and we have evidence to show that every time something goes bad, if we take care of the customer, they will have a longer lifetime value than the average one.

The cost of replacing the product for free, or whatever else it takes to make the customer happy, is minimal compared to the return on investment. In our early years, we didn't have the data to bear this out. We simply had an assertion and a conviction that it was the right thing to do, and we stayed the course. It was a leap of faith, really.

Today, we have data to prove it. We measure what we call "downstream impact," which is "If we do something for the customer today, how does that customer behave twelve months or eighteen months down the road, and beyond?" And loyalty and/or the long-term value of that affected customer comes in at anywhere from 2× to 5×.

So if the long-term value of an average customer is, say, $200, we've found that the long-term value of a customer who's experienced some sort of dissatisfaction with our service only to have that negative experience then addressed in a positive way—that customer will be worth anywhere from $400 to $1,000 in value over the next twelve to eighteen months.

It's no longer a leap of faith. It isn't a guess. Doing the right thing, going above and beyond to correct a mistake or perceived error and give the customer the most satisfying, WOW-worthy experience we can, yields two to five times in customer value.

WOW, right?

This data has only become available to us internally in the last two to three years, and with this book, we're just starting to share it with the world. If there's anything that's been holding companies back from

> *Doing the right thing, going above and beyond to correct a mistake or perceived error and give the customer the most satisfying, WOW-worthy experience we can, yields two to five times in customer value.*

embracing a better customer service model, and a service-first mentality from top to bottom, I think it's because up until now it really has been something intangible. But if we can get business leaders to see this data, my hope is that we'll also see a broader shift toward better service across a wide spectrum of businesses.

Why wouldn't any company want to increase customer value two to five times while simultaneously improving everyone's experience on both sides of the equation?

And that 2× to 5× number is only the beginning. Most of the customers who experience the Zappos brand of customer service interaction turn into a segment that we call "lovers." They become brand lovers. And once they're "lovers," they rarely defect. They rarely churn out of pocket. They come back again and again. They become advocates for our brand. They become our best customers, often for life.

That's powerful. And it's very, very real.

Megan Petrini
Onboarding
My team and I like to watch Forensic Files *while prepping in between new-hire training classes.*

It's amazing to think that we have the data to back up our decision-making now, especially knowing that we were making the decision to treat every customer—even the questionable customers—really, really well, going all the way back to the beginning.

I first started in 2006. I was hired for the phones and loved, loved, loved it. In six months, I moved to the resource desk, which is one of our specialty teams that helps out our phone reps, as well as handles sensitive customer situations.

A few weeks into that new position, one of our brand-new hires came up to me in tears. So I was immediately defensive, like, "Who made you cry? Send that call to me, right now!"

At that time, we were in the habit of giving out dollars-off coupons for lost service when something went wrong. They were good for one time only, and then they were gone. Use them or lose them kind of thing.

This particular customer had been given a $50-off coupon maybe a year or two earlier. A really long time ago. And she placed an order. She used the coupon. And then she returned the order and ordered something else and tried to use the coupon again. It didn't work. So she called in and said she was really disappointed because she "didn't realize" that the coupon was only good one time. Our CLT member did what we tend to do here at Zappos: She gave her the benefit of the doubt. She said, "Oh, yeah. I'm so sorry. It's supposed to be for one-time use, but let me go ahead and just replace it for you, and now you *know* it's just for one-time use."

This customer then placed a new order, used the new coupon, then returned the order, and did the same thing all over again. We tried to tell her no, but she got upset, and the next representative gave her a new coupon, too.

It turned out she had done this five or six times. She was abusing our kindness. So when our new hire passed that call to me, I was like, "No. Nuh-uh. Not today."

I was very friendly, but I was firm: "I'm sorry, but we're not going to be able to do this again. The answer is no. You've been told many times we're not going to do it again, and it's become abusive. The answer is no."

And she said, "Well, I'm never gonna shop here again."

"Well," I said, "I'm sorry you feel that way."

I didn't know at the time, but that wasn't the Zappos way. It was a knee-jerk response, and I cringe just thinking about it now.

"I'm gonna email your CEO!" the customer said.

And I was like, "The email for Tony is . . ." and I gave her his email address. I was 100 percent sure I was in the right.

I hung up the phone feeling proud of myself for shutting her down, figuring we would never hear from her again. I went home, came back the next day and walked to my computer, and I saw a Post-it note on my screen. It was from Tony Hsieh.

He said, "Give her the coupon."

Just imagine how positive and big I felt at *that* moment. Not at all. I had to call her back, and I had to apologize. She just ate it up the whole time. She was so nasty to me. But I had to take it because I *was* completely in the wrong. And that was when I learned the hard way the very same lesson that I teach to all of our new hires: Our job isn't to protect Zappos from the customer. We are not the Zappos police! Our job is to provide the Zappos experience. We only talk to a fraction of our active customer base, which numbers in the tens of millions. It's a tiny percentage of that already tiny percentage who try to abuse the system. We have the opportunity every time that we talk to somebody, to turn that person into a great customer, the best customer, just by giving them a positive experience. It's not our job to cause an escalation. It's not our job to protect the company. It's our job to provide the Zappos experience.

> **Make the best decision for the customer—because the best decision for the customer is always the best decision for the company.**

So what if this woman was ripping us off $50 at a time. Who cares? We're not going broke because of this one lady and her $50 coupons. Eventually she stopped doing it. And it's probably the escalation that was the last straw for her—but instead of sticking around, she took her business elsewhere and probably complained about her experience with us.

In today's world we are so ingrained to immediately be defensive, to want to make our point, to win, to be the police of whatever, you know?

Don't do it.

When I tell this story in class there are always people who've come from different call centers, or different finance jobs, and they ask, "Okay, what if . . . ?" And my answer is, "Nope, doesn't matter."

"But what if . . . ?"

"Nope, doesn't matter."

In this case, the woman wasn't costing us very much, because she was just buying things and then returning them. And buying and returning. Eventually, she weeded herself out. It wasn't a huge deal. But I made it a big deal when I didn't need to—and that didn't benefit the company or anyone else.

So the customer-service lesson of the day is this: Make the best decision for the customer, and then let it go. Not the best decision for the company or your ego or anything else.

Make the best decision for the customer—because the best decision for the customer is always the best decision for the company.

Arun Rajan
Chief Operating Officer
My wife and kids love dogs. I don't.

Our method isn't foolproof. We do have some people who abuse our kindness, who try to get freebies and perks that aren't warranted. It happens. And there have been some really egregious cases where we've had to cut a customer off and politely ask them to take their business elsewhere. But those cases are truly the exceptions, and when you net it out, our approach to keep catering to the vast majority of customers who are *not* trying to rip us off is massively profitable. So we're going to keep doing that.

If we changed our model to cater to the exceptions, if we took away our CLT's ability to truly WOW with service, we could probably shave a few million bucks off the budget next year, right? But that is incredibly short-term thinking. It wouldn't make any sense. We'd wind up losing much more than we gained because we would lose the core value of our brand. That erosion of what we do best would lead us to lose our Zappos brand lovers, as well as our ability to create new brand lovers in the process.

How could that be considered a win for anyone?

Especially when you consider that focusing on the positive not only feels better but is better for business.

BEYOND PROFITS

Jesse Juhala
Representative, Dynamic Customer Service

Last year, right after I got on the floor, I received
a call from a lady asking about a pair of cowboy
boots she had already bought from us once before.
I looked them up and let her know we only had the
next size up. She said that would work "okay."

Since she had just ordered the same boots a few
months earlier, I decided to probe a bit and asked
if there was something wrong with those boots.
That was when she tearfully told me that three

days earlier, she had lost her dream home in a fire. She and her husband had built it themselves after they retired, and in addition to the home, they lost two vehicles, several cats and dogs, a horse, and pretty much everything they owned.

To make matters worse, a couple days after the fire broke out, some looters opened up their fireproof safe and stole everything in it. I had tears coming down my face as she told me all of this, and repeatedly told her how sorry I was. In the end, I gave her the boots for free. It was something small, but I just wanted her to have something so she could at least *begin* to rebuild her life.

She started bawling. She was so thankful.

After the call I kept thinking how that just didn't seem like enough. I approached one of my team members here and we started brainstorming ideas. In the end we got our resident artist, Miguel, to paint a picture of her house on a pine box, and we filled the box with a gas card, a Zappos gift certificate (so her husband could buy some shoes if he wanted), and a gift certificate for a local restaurant so they could have a night out and not think about what happened. We also included a hand-painted card signed by everyone who helped out.

I wish I could have done more for them. But it was something. I wanted those people to know that what they went through wasn't lost on us. We were all here wishing them the best as they recovered from such a terrible loss.

Stevie Bautista
Head of Employee Engagement and
Zappos for Good
My favorite food is sugar gummy worms.

Jesse's desire to connect, to give, to do something for someone else is something we see with so many of our employees. And that's something that we strive to embrace here at Zappos, on all sorts of levels.

There are plenty of businesses that give money to charity and various causes. I don't think it's a coincidence that some of the most recognizable brands in the world, in a wide variety of industries, are also some of the most charitable. Walmart, Coca-Cola, Goldman Sachs, Target, even Exxon Mobil give tens of millions, if not hundreds of millions, of dollars in donations to various causes every year. It's clearly good for business. It's good for PR. It's good for the community, the country, the environment, and the whole world, in some cases.

We can't compete with that level of giving here at Zappos. Even if we could, what we really like to do is to make giving a part of the Zappos experience.

It's funny because when I first started, I worked in employee relations, and I wound up being the guy who was in charge of firing people. (Yes, we sometimes have to fire people at Zappos, just like any other business. And for many of the same reasons as one might find anywhere else.) My nickname internally was "Grim Reaper." Not exactly a title I loved! So I moved over to the charitable side of things, where Zappos was already in the process of throwing everything standard about "giving" out the window and starting from scratch, to build something that really fit our culture. A team called Zappos for Good.

Looking to our core values, we really wanted to focus on the idea of "How do we engage employees, and how do we make it something that's really fun, but at the same time we're doing a lot of good?"

We decided the best thing to do would be to start in our own back yard. To hold events right on our campus grounds in Downtown Las Vegas, and we started with the most fitting holiday, Thanksgiving. We worked with local charitable organizations to invite 750 families to come in and get Thanksgiving dinners they could take home with them. But because we're a company focused on experiences, we wanted it to be much more than a handout. We planned how the kids could have fun when they came here, setting up a petting zoo and games. The whole event was set up and staffed by our own employees on a completely voluntary basis, and we had so many volunteers we had to rotate them in shifts just to accommodate everyone. It was a huge success. And we turned to the staff when it was over and asked them for suggestions for other community events, and we've been doing about ten major events like that on campus every year since. Almost one per month.

People really do love to be a part of something that feels good, and to know that it's authentic.

One of the bigger events that we did was for a local zoo. We had an employee who was working to save a mom-and-pop zoo that had been around for more than a decade from going out of business. This employee had raised about $10,000 on a GoFundMe page, which was great. But the zoo needed more like $250,000 to survive. So within a two-week period we brought the eighty-animal menagerie to Zappos and actually turned the whole campus into a zoo for a weekend. We invited the public, charged admission, and asked for donations, and we raised about $151,000. In a weekend!

If we had any doubts about whether connecting employees to the local community could have real results, they went out the window after that. We've since done Easter dinner days, complete with visits from the Easter Bunny and all sorts of rides and games, and it's been great for everyone. We're overstaffed with volunteers at every event, so clearly we're doing something that our employees believe in, and there's no doubt our events have been loved and embraced by the Las Vegas community as well.

I think part of the reason it's been so successful is because it's not done for PR. My department isn't tied to marketing at all. We're actually organized under HR, because we see this more as a benefit and a boost for employees as much as anything else. People really do love to be a part of something that feels good, and to know that it's authentic. We aren't looking for media coverage (although we get some whether we try to or not) and certainly aren't looking for the most impressions.

It's more inspiring for the employee to see a company doing something like this because it's the right thing to do and not as a way to bring cameras around all the time. It gives our employees an extra sense of pride in the company for which they work. And it's a point of pride for the company itself as well.

It's not inexpensive. At our prom event, a thousand kids come in and pick out free prom dresses and shoes and accessories and tuxedos, all courtesy of Zappos. There is no direct return on investment on any of that beyond the pride and the good feeling we're spreading in our community. But this isn't a numbers-driven part of the business. It's about our values. It's about our desire to make the world a little better—even just our little corner of the world. And I don't think there's an employee here who hasn't been touched in one way or another by working those events.

It just further feeds our employees' desire to connect and give. And then you see that spirit get reflected in all sorts of ways, in all sorts of interactions around here, every day.

Jeanne Markel
Technical Advisor to CEO Tony Hsieh
I met my husband on the side of the road three decades ago—my car was broken down and he stopped to help.

I'm proud that the spirit of service carries over into everything we do, from the time and attention we show customers on the phone, to the small gifts we give to recognize our coworkers, the items or money we donate to charitable causes, and the ways we give back to our community. We truly strive to provide everybody with the same WOW-worthy experience, which guides not only how we treat our customers but also how we interact with each other, our vendors, and members of our downtown community.

What's been proven over these last twenty years is that creating this service-first culture has benefits that extend far beyond what you might imagine. It actually creates the kind of culture that businesses need to grow, to adapt, to retain employees for longer periods of time, and to survive in an ever-changing world. There are all sorts of positive benefits that come out of our core values and core mindset, and there are actual numbers to back it up now. Being humble is important to us, but there's a certain amount of success here that simply can't be denied.

Of course, we have to continue to deliver profits while we're doing all of these other good things. People wrongly assume it's some sort of an uphill challenge, but we're showing that it's the good things that are actually *sustaining* our profitability over a long period of time. We're not losing something by doing these things. We're not cutting into our profits in any significant way to give back to the community. Instead, we're working even harder to create a system that benefits everyone, all at once.

In business, relationships matter. When a vendor comes to town, we pick them up at the airport and, though we are the customer, we fight to pay the lunch or dinner check. At meetings, we show them all their sales and profit margins figures, in full transparency. If we have a really great season, we're showing it to them. And if we have a really terrible season, we're also showing it to them. It's not because of a demand for them to contribute to our margins to make up for the numbers we didn't hit. It's because we are full partners, and we both have a stake in our successes and failures— and in open communication.

Having a service-first mindset creates the kind of culture that businesses need to grow, to adapt, to retain employees for longer periods of time, and to survive in an ever-changing world.

We're not trying to rip you off to make us better. Instead, it's "Let's work together. Let's build a *real* partnership. Let's sell lots of your product, because we like your product and we want to make you look good, and obviously we want to be profitable, too."

I think about our interactions with the larger brands over the years, and how representatives of those brands have become some of the closest friends that I have, and no doubt will continue to be even though I'm out of the merchandising realm now. For me, developing those friendships was pretty incredible.

Eileen Tetreault, Mike Normart, and Scott Julian
Merchandising

MIKE We had a rep that we worked with, from one of our vendors, and he had been in the industry for I don't know how many years.

EILEEN Fifty? At least?

MIKE At least. He really helped us in the early days. Going all the way back to our first round, when we had a real tough time convincing brands to sell to this unknown start-up. Anyway, he believed in us. And he was just a good guy. He'd been in the industry forever, and everybody knew him, so when he retired, we threw a big dinner for him.

SCOTT We made a picture book for him and had people sign it. And we gave him a big fishing pole and a golf putter—

MIKE And at the end of the night he said, "You know, my own company didn't even do this."

SCOTT Is that even a surprise, though? He'd been there for decades, but companies don't really value that sort of loyalty anymore. In most places, when you retire, you're lucky if they get you a cake to share in the conference room on your way out.

 EILEEN We didn't even think about any of that. We just wanted to treat and honor the guy, so we put a little movie together for him. It was a really nice night.

MIKE He sends us postcards now when he's touring Europe. He goes, "Yeah, I'm on vacation!" It's awesome.

SCOTT I have to say, it's pretty great to work for a place where you're free to treat people like they ought to be treated—even when they're not an employee, and even when there's nothing to gain from them in return. It just feels right.

Hollie Delaney
Chief Human Resources Officer
I got my first tattoo at forty years old.

Infusing some humanity into the work we do creates a positive outcome in terms of customer service. We've proven that again and again.

Other companies have proven it, too. Look at any list of America's Best Companies, and especially Best Places to Work, and you'll find examples of policies that treat people like people, and benefits that support employee education and family leave time and more. It's not a coincidence that those companies are usually super successful. Look at companies like TOMS Shoes, which gives away a pair of shoes to someone in need for every pair they sell, or so many others that attempt to do good in the world and involve their employees in doing good while they're at it. There are hundreds, maybe thousands, of heartwarming stories out there, just like the ones you've been reading from Zappos, that involve customers and vendors and charities and more.

> *Maybe it's not broken, but maybe there's a better way to do something. If it's not broken, break it. See if and how you can break it . . . That's when change happens. That's when growth happens.*

Work should be about more than making profits. Your job isn't just "I did what somebody else told me to do that kept this company running and made my bosses and shareholders a lot of money." At least, it shouldn't be. At Zappos, we want to open our minds, to do things that make a difference, to make real, *purposeful* change in the company, in our city, and in the world.

One thing people say in workplaces all the time is, "If it ain't broke, don't fix it." Well, first, you might be *saying* it's not broken when it actually is. And second, if you never reexamine something, you'll never have any advancement. If people had just said, "Oh, I can add things up myself and I can write out my report by hand. It's not broken!" then we wouldn't have calculators or computers. We wouldn't have any new technologies. We'd still be riding horses to work.

When it comes to the workplace, just as with anything else, it's important every now and then—or maybe even all the time— to say, "Maybe it's not broken, but maybe there's a better way to do something."

In other words: If it's not broken, *break it*. See if and how you *can* break it. If you actually can't break it, maybe you don't change it. But the thing we've found here at Zappos is you can break pretty much everything. And when you do that, when you stop being complacent, great things can happen. That's when change happens. That's when growth happens. That's when bigger things than you ever imagined possible start to happen—starting with the growth that sprouts from your very own employees.

PART II

Cultivating

BELOW
THE SURFACE

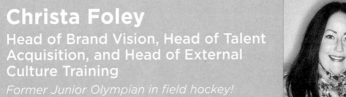

Christa Foley

Head of Brand Vision, Head of Talent Acquisition, and Head of External Culture Training

Former Junior Olympian in field hockey! Look it up—it's not lacrosse like you might be thinking. ☺

When you trust your employees, when you share their core values, when everything you do together comes from a place of service, you find that you can give them a lot of leeway. You can let them break out of their boxes. Encourage them to try new things. Share in their unique and original ideas, and discover their own unique talents.

And that's when they can surprise you—because what you see is often just the tip of the iceberg. Someone you hired for one thing might actually be better at something else. In fact, they might be really *great* at something else. And the results that come from that trust, that letting go, from knowing that it's okay to encourage people to grow and change right under your own roof, can be much bigger than you ever expect.

Johnnie Brockett
Treasury and Accounts Receivable
I own more shoes now than I have in my whole life combined.

I'm in the Treasury department. So I manage the company's money, pay all the bills, taxes, payroll, resolutions, anything dealing with money. I oversee tens of millions of dollars in transactions every week. And as I mentioned earlier, I came here with zero financial background. Zero years of college. (And, thankfully, zero student loans.)

How does that happen?

When I came to Zappos, I started on the phones. I had come from the retention department of another company where every caller was really angry, and the place just wasn't run right, so I embraced the fact that I was empowered here to fix people's problems. People's packages got left out in the rain, or we sent them the wrong size, or what have you. Things happen. Callers can get angry. But we're allowed and encouraged to really do anything it takes to make things right for the customer, as long as we don't break the company. It felt really good to be able to do that, to literally make people's days, to save a wedding, or to save an event for a customer.

I was proud of the work I did from day one, and I think that made me want to work even harder. Other people here saw that.

They saw how hard I worked. They noticed. And they did something about it.

After only three or four months, they promoted me to R-Desk, the resource desk, which handles sensitive customer situations. Then I became a "team lead," which is like a manager. And then they liked what I was doing so much, they wanted me to find other people with my kind of enthusiasm and work ethic, so I spent some time working with recruiting. When I wanted a change, they saw the people skills I had and they moved me to merchandising. Then I got to move to finance, and I'm literally 95 percent self-taught. At Zappos, if you work hard and get the job done, it doesn't matter what your background is. They care about who you are as a person. They care about your work ethic. They care that you care.

Clearly, I don't mind working, especially when I love the work I do. I never got anywhere just for being a snappy dresser.

I actually got into finance through Zappos' internal internship program. Our internships are ninety days. Usually you go, you do the job, make sure you like it and you can do it efficiently, and make sure you match with the team. You have to fit. They liked me. So my ninety days became 120, then 150, then 180. And the whole time they were trying to find me a job, but it was hard. Seven months later they pulled me into a room and said, "We found a job for you." There was an opening on the Treasury team because the guy that was on the team at that point wanted to move and do something else. So I replaced him. I trained. And right after that, my boss had some family stuff happen so he went out on leave. Overnight it was basically me and this kid barely out of college running the Treasury department.

It was crazy. I had to learn by doing. But I always felt supported here. I just double-checked everything about six times before anything happened, you know? And I'm proud to say that since I got on the team in April of 2017 until today, I've made $1.24

in mistakes. I'd rather be perfect, but nobody's perfect, so $1.24 seems acceptable.

It's funny to think that maybe I was meant for this job and just never knew it. There are talented people all over this country who are working, who hate their jobs, who are bored to death, who aren't being used to their full—forget their *full* potential, just to *any* potential. They're filling a role, reading a script on a phone on a telemarketing thing or whatever it might be, and their potential is never tapped. What if we tapped everyone's potential? Can you imagine what these employees could become?

I look at my own life, and the ways I've changed personally, and it's really something. I didn't think I was going to live to be eighteen years old, the way I was operating.

I'm not living that life anymore. Sunday nights I don't do anything. All my friends go to the club, but I have meetings on Monday and I have to come to work. I have stuff to do. So I don't do anything on Sundays. I have this job and people depend on me.

This company took a chance on me, and I've learned that this company is willing to take chances all the time. That's what makes it great. If somebody fails, the attitude is "Hey, you're not gonna win every time—but you're definitely not gonna win if you don't try something." It's the kind of thing coaches teach, and life coaches teach, and motivational speakers teach, but so many companies don't practice it. They're too scared. And I mean, I get it. A lot of companies might not be in a position to take million-dollar risks. We're lucky that we can. But we only got here by taking smaller risks along the way, including risks on employees who wanted to do more than whatever they were first hired to do. We just go for it. We do what feels right.

Matt Thomas
Merchandising

I have two rescued chihuahuas. One has three legs and one eye.

I just had my ten-year anniversary, and it's been a pretty cool ride here. I guess even before I started with Zappos, it was kind of weird how I found out about the company. I worked for a heavy equipment rental agency, writing for their training manuals and stuff—it was so boring—and our editor, she brought in the Zappos Culture Book from 2005. And she said, "I want you guys to read this book."

The Culture Book was basically a collection of stories from Zappos employees (not unlike a few of the little anecdotal stories you're reading in these pages), but I had no idea what Zappos was. So I asked.

"They sell shoes and handbags," she said.

I was twenty-five. I said, "I'm not into those. I don't care. I just wear the same pair of sneakers and t-shirts and whatever," and she said, "Just read it. You don't have to read the whole thing."

I started reading it that night, and it was enthralling. I'm reading about these people who love what they do, and love their work, and nobody had anything negative to say about anybody and I thought, *This is not how I pictured business*. I thought every single business everywhere was just like Gordon Gekko from *Wall Street*. Cutthroat. Greedy.

So the next day, I walked in and told the editor, "I read it front to back."

"That's great. What can we incorporate into our area here?" she asked.

"I don't think we can do that with the current culture here. It's not possible," I said. "So I'm gonna resign." I handed her my Blackberry.

"Do you have, like, anything lined up?" she asked me.

"No, I'm just gonna go work there," I said.

I hadn't even contacted Zappos before I quit. But I felt this huge relief resigning from that job. I called Zappos and was told I had to apply online, so I did. I applied for a CLT job. My aunt told me, "Put some mantras on your résumé," things like "Work hard, play harder" and other stuff that described me as a person. I thought it was kind of dumb, but I did it. And it worked. Jacob Palmer, a recruiter at Zappos, called me. He was like, "Hey, we got your résumé. Love the mantras!"

They brought me in and gave me a technical test, which was really easy. It was basically online shopping and putting things into shopping carts, which apparently a lot of applicants couldn't do in 2007, but I did fine. And I happened to find a "caching error" on one of the pages, and I mentioned it, which Jacob said showed "great attention to detail."

I applied for a couple of different positions, including a content job, but after getting the whole tour of the company and everything, it didn't matter what position I got hired for—I was fully on board. What I wanted more than anything was just to work for this cool company, to take a graveyard shift on the phones—because I was just out of college and staying up until three in the morning most nights anyway—and nothing else.

I was happy.

Eventually they moved me into the content department where I did a bunch of different things. Then my friend Jeff, who was on the content team, moved to merchandising and said, "This is a great gig. We were looking at product, we were talking about it, we were learning about it. We just are *buying* it now instead of writing about it."

I told him I wasn't interested. I was happy working forty-hour weeks with less pressure. I heard stories of merchants working eighty-hour weeks. *No way!* I had no ambition to do anything like that.

Then one day, Tom, one of Zappos' first vendors and our sales representative for Clarks, which was one of our first big brands, invited me to come to the Zalloween charity golf tournament that October. I wrote descriptions for Clarks, and we had talked about golf a bit, and he said, "We have an open spot. I know you like to golf," and I said, "Okay, sounds fun."

So I went to the golf tournament and right when I was about to put my golf shoes on I found a dead mouse in one of them. Yuck—I guess I hadn't golfed in a while. But I had no other golf shoes, so I put this shoe on, and I was so grossed out that I was busy thinking about this dead mouse when Tom introduced me to our team.

"We're playing with Fred, Steve, Galen, Jeanne," he said. These were all bigwigs who had been at the company forever. The only one I knew and had any relationship with was Jeanne because she was the Director of Casual Lifestyle. She had kind of hinted to me to try merchandising, too, and I had told her, "I don't know, not my thing."

So we played. We teed off, and I guess because my mind was still on the mouse, I wasn't overthinking anything—and I just crushed it, right off the bat. Everyone on the team was like, "You play golf!"

"Golf plays me," I said, "but I've played some, yes."

I sank a 45-foot putt on the second hole, and Jeanne was like, "You're hired. You're hired. You're gonna come work for me."

"I didn't apply," I said.

I really didn't think she was serious. But then half a round later, Galen, who I really didn't know at that point, said, "Hey, you know we have a job opening. And specifically, you'd be buying golf apparel. You obviously play golf. This would be a great job for you. I can see Jeanne wants you to work for her, and I trust her judgment, so you should really consider this."

"Wow," I said. "Like, that's—WOW!"

I couldn't believe it.

I spoke to Jeff, and I was just honest. I said, "Jeff, I'm so scared. But I know I can't let fear run my life, and this sounds cool. It sounds like a dream job for a lot of people. Maybe it's *my* dream job—so I'm gonna do it. I'll interview with people and I wanna do this!"

I talked myself into it!

I interviewed with a bunch of different people and they hired me on the growing clothing team as a merchandise assistant. And as soon as I started, I just loved it. It was intense. I was working all the time—unlimited overtime. But within a month I was making business decisions that were tens of thousands of dollars. Zappos gave me free rein: "Just do whatever you want to do." They trusted me to follow my gut and instincts, and to use my experience as a golfer. Six months into it I truly loved what I was doing, but I was freaking out over the pace of it all. *I can't keep track of all this*, I said to myself.

One day, Terry, my boss whom I had known since new-hire training, pulled me into a room, and I thought that he was going to terminate me, because I felt like I wasn't doing enough.

But Terry, my friend, said, "No, dude, we're gonna promote you! You're doing a great job, and we want to reward you for that."

That was seven years ago. Seven years later, I've seen the company quadruple in size in the corporate headquarters, and I'm still here. And it's kind of weird to think about. I really didn't have any ambition, but Zappos pulled that out of me. I just wanted to work graveyard at this fun company. That was all I wanted to do! But people give you opportunities here and present things to you. At other companies, if you're a buyer, you come into the job as a buyer and you'll probably stay at that job as a buyer, and maybe retire from that job as a buyer. It's very challenging to move around in other companies. But here, everybody intermingles. Relationships are built across departments. From the training on up, you have friendships. I had friends in merchandising with whom I trained in the very beginning, which made it so much easier to take that leap. And the relationship building I did here was a great model for what I wanted to do in my new role, too. I've always thought of working at Zappos as "I help make the world a better place because I help people be happy."

If I buy the right products, and people come here and find something they can love, that's retail therapy! I'm helping them be happy. It's not saving babies, but it's still spreading joy, right? (The really crazy thing is, we did save babies! With money we've raised through the Zalloween charity golf event, we've actually helped two women through difficult pregnancies. So we've saved babies.)

I've always thought of working at Zappos as "I help make the world a better place because I help people be happy."

I'm in charge of that Zalloween tournament now, which is a challenge that I never would have imagined for myself. It's a big golf tournament. It's like planning a wedding every year. But it's fun. And none of that would have happened if Zappos wasn't built the way it's built, to support its employees and see them for who they are, and to give them opportunities to express who they are through their work.

I've watched my friends progress here, too, and that's just super rewarding. Some of them have climbed a lot higher than me, but I don't feel jealous or envious. I want to see them succeed. Their success is *my* success. Watching an employee grow, I feel like a proud parent. I'm just like so flipping excited that they are growing as people.

We have rivalries. But they're lighthearted. We joke around about business, and we push people to be better. We all go through the same trials and tribulations, albeit at different levels. We have a shared experience that brings us together, and we're able to give advice to each other, like, "Oh, maybe if you try this or try that . . . this is what I've done . . ."

It's all about working together. The golden rule for all Zappos merchants, as it is in HR, is you treat people as you want to be treated.

And the great lesson in that is: You don't have to be savage to succeed.

Tyler Williams
Head of Brand Aura
Watched the entire series of Smallville *twice (217 episodes each time).*

By eight years old, I 100 percent knew I was going to be a rock star.

Of course, until you're a full-blown rock star, being a musician doesn't pay very well. So once I was out of school I had to hold down "real" jobs on the side. I did things from inspecting oil tanks in Alaska, to construction, to production, but I always had this fascination with how things work, tinkering and building things. When I was in a band, I would build the set pieces and the lighting design and sound, and I learned how to record the band, and I would help with social media.

One of the things I've always believed is that musicians are sometimes the ultimate entrepreneurs because they have to be. They put tens of thousands of hours into practice; they have to manage personal relationships that are highly emotional within the group, a bunch of artists. You have to risk everything, hop in a van, raise money, beg, borrow, steal, whatever, to get your music into people's hands all while knowing that you have a one-in-a-million chance of ever making it. But that doesn't stop them from marketing themselves and creating a product and investing their personal time and money into that product and getting other people to invest their personal time and money into all of that, too.

As a musician, I think I naturally just picked up a lot of that entrepreneurial mindset, or maybe I had it from the onset and I didn't recognize what it was. But I was never afraid to put it all out there and risk it.

Before I found Zappos, I was touring with a band, and it was actually a good job. I was making good money as a drummer. I was a hired gun in a touring band. But when EMI and Universal merged, the band got dropped from the label. So I came back home after spending four years on the road feeling all burned out, and I told my wife, "I'm kinda over this. Like, maybe I can find a good gig in Las Vegas." Las Vegas is a great town for musicians. I knew somebody at the Blue Man Group, and I went and did an audition and I was probably going to get hired to be their background drummer. Not as a Blue Man, but as a drummer in their band. And my wife came home that day, and she said, "Hey, I took a tour of a business today. I think you should check them out."

She said she met the company's "life coach" and the head of HR and she said, "Everybody was laughing and having a good time and people were playing jokes on each other." And then she said—these were her words—"It was like an adult daycare I would feel comfortable dropping you off at!"

First of all, I'm not sure what that says about having a drummer for a husband. But second, it sounded pretty cool! I'd never heard any workplace described that way. I had never heard of Zappos. So I checked it out. I googled it and hopped on YouTube, and Tony had just dropped *Delivering Happiness* into bookstores, so I picked it up. I just really connected to that message of delivering happiness. I connected with the Ten Core Values.

On the website, it said they needed a résumé, a job history, all of the typical stuff, and I was like, "Damn. I barely graduated high school, never went to college, plus I've been touring in a band the last four years as a contractor so I have *no* job history." What was I going to tell them? "I'm a drummer?"

And then I read a statistic that said it was harder to get into Zappos than it was to get into Harvard, and I was really discouraged.

It wasn't until I noticed that they had an option to include a video cover letter on the job application that I thought I might have a shot. A video I could do. *That's the only way I am going to stand out*, I thought, *because my résumé blows.*

My wife encouraged me. She said, "You know what? Their core values are important. Why don't you use your creativity and write a song about them?" So that was what I did. It snowballed into this crazy project that took about three weeks, where I worked in a studio with a green screen and I created a song based on the Ten Core Values, recorded it, and made a video, which had like eight of me dancing and singing and playing all the instruments. It was beyond ridiculous, but I sent it in. And literally within five minutes of sending it I got a call from Michael, then the manager of Recruiting, saying, "Hey, we don't really have a position for you, but come down here because we want to meet you and figure something out!"

I remember watching the video when Tyler submitted it online, and I loved it and forwarded it to Christa. Check it out here: https://youtu.be/6uevQOLYMBo.

—TONY

So I went down, and he put me together with the AV team. They had an opening in their department, but they let me know right away that it couldn't be mine. "Your video is great but, just so you know, we're not going to go with you," they said. "We like to hire from within and we have somebody in CLT whom we've had our eye on and has been here a while and we want to give them the opportunity." They didn't know me yet, they said, and didn't know if I was a culture fit, so they really showed me how much they valued culture over qualification.

I was bummed out, but I was also hooked. Like, "Wow, this company is legit. They practice what they preach."

I was walking out to the parking lot and Kari, who was in HR at the time, ran out, and she was like, "Hey, bummer you didn't get the AV position, but would you be willing to start on the phones?" And I was like, "Yeah!"

If CLT was the *first* thing they offered, I would have been excited. So I started on the phones, loved it, and then slowly worked my way to being an intern in the training program. I was training other people coming into the company. Loved that. I did that for a year, and then my internship was up and I was kind of at this crossroads. And throughout the first couple years of my journey at Zappos, people found out that I was good at certain things. Like, I could build a Halloween float or I could help with power distribution at events. I just volunteered for everything I could.

When they hired production teams to do lighting for an event, people would come to me to scrub the contracts and see if the pricing seemed fair. I just became a source for a bunch of different things that weren't under my job description in CLT. And then the pinnacle change was when I got an email from Tony's "time ninja," as people called her, his assistant, Liz. She said, "We have an emergency. Tony's speaking for Amazon and Disney and a bunch of executives at his apartment tonight and nobody sourced AV," meaning he didn't have a microphone, a projector, anything. "We're in a bind."

I came to the rescue.

At the time, Tony's apartment then was in the Ogden, and it was really three apartments with the walls knocked out between them.

It had three kitchens, three living rooms, three sets of bedrooms, like a big maze, and they had no idea how to get audio to people all over the apartment, and I said, "Oh, I've got it. No problem."

> *I moved out of my apartment at the Ogden in 2014, and now live in an Airstream trailer. It's part of a renovated hotel that's been turned into a combination of a public community gathering space and private residential. As I'm writing this, I live with thirty residents in Airstreams and Tumbleweed Tiny Houses, fifteen dogs, five cats, and a free-roaming alpaca named Marley, with a campfire going every night next to the community kitchen, barbecue area, and pool. People ask how I can live in such a tiny space, but I feel like I have the world's largest living room and backyard, and anytime I go outside, there is always something going on and interesting people to talk to.*

Tony

I set him up, ran sound, did the video, did everything wirelessly so I didn't have to run cable everywhere. And Jamie Naughton, who is Chief of Staff, came up to me and said, "Hey, your name keeps coming up. You're helping out on all these things, and then you came here tonight in your off time to do this. Like, who are you and what is your deal?" We chatted for a couple hours, and at the end she asked me, "If you could do anything, what would you want to do?"

I told her I wanted to do all of this different stuff I was doing on the side, but more of it.

"Can you write that into a job description and name it, title it, tell us what you want to get paid, and send it over?" she said.

I was like, "Okay!"

So I came up with a term that I thought covered all of the various things that I had been up to: "Fungineer!" I wrote up a dream job description along with what I thought was an appropriate salary ask, and I sent it over to her. In a couple days she wrote back, "This is approved. You're now the Fungineer."

What other company would do something like that?

I wound up doing all of the things I'd been doing on the side, only full time, helping set up our All-Hands Meetings (where we put everyone in the company in one auditorium for a cool presentation and update on everything Zappos once every quarter) and all sorts of internally focused projects. But more and more I kept getting tapped on the experimental marketing side of things, too, including one day when Kelly's team said, "Hey, Tyler, could you build the Red Bull Flugtag for us?" So I went to Portland and built an aircraft for the Flugtag, which is basically a hang-glider competition featuring a bunch of amateurs who don't know how to build hang-gliders. Ours did not glide and we went down in flames, but it looked cool while we did it, so it was a hit. And then Tony started actually tapping me for a lot of his personal projects. He's big on experiments, such as "What if we built a jacket that had charging ports in it with batteries?" So I built him one. It was a prototype, a piece of crap with wires hanging everywhere, but it worked.

This was right after Tony sold the company to Amazon, and he did something pretty amazing with that sale. He asked to be paid all up front, so there were no stock options that would vest over time. And then he asked to only be paid $36,000 a year, so he had no golden handcuffs—meaning he's not incentivized to maximize profits. Tony is technically donating his time to Zappos because he pays for all his own meals, entertainment, and travel, which nets out to a loss to him personally. It was kind of brilliant, because it allowed him the freedom to work on things he was passionate about at Zappos.

The deal Tony made with Amazon stipulated that he could run Zappos in his own unique way, as long as we achieved our mutually agreed upon success metrics. He also created a budget called "Brand Aura," which he controlled. This budget was earmarked for experimental projects that didn't require a direct ROI attached to them. I was constantly tapping into that budget—not only for his ideas, but also for my own. I would come up with ideas, like "Hey, we should put music in the plaza" or "We should put some grass in for a dog park on campus," and he would fund the things out of that budget.

Finally, Tony, who was dedicating quite a bit of his time to DTP Companies, just said, "Hey, do you want to just take over the Brand Aura budget? Because I trust you, I think you have good ideas, and I don't have the time to really manage that fund appropriately."

DTP Companies, formerly known as Downtown Project, is a separate organization personally funded by myself and some other early Zappos employees that is focused on helping revitalize Downtown Vegas. More than $350 million has been invested in real estate, small businesses, tech start-ups, education, art, and music festivals to help create a walkable neighborhood that is a place of inspiration, creativity, entrepreneurial energy, upward mobility, and discovery.

TONY

Remember, I'm the drummer guy. With no résumé. Who started on the phones.

"Sure!" I said, not having a clue what I was getting myself into.

When I took over this budget, there were only a couple of months left in the year, and there was a lot of money left on the table. So we decided to take something we'd done on campus and turn it into a nationwide event: pet adoptions. Those pet adoption parties were such a great big feel-good hit on campus, we thought, "How great would it be for the brand if we could deliver that kind of happiness to a whole bunch of different communities? And how great would it be to find a whole bunch of pets new homes between now and Christmas?"

Everybody rallied behind it—a huge thanks to my fellow Zapponians like Stevie and a million other passionate people. The company really loved the initiative, and so did the public. We were trending on Facebook and getting all sorts of love online for what we were doing. The adoption organizations received a bunch of attention and additional donations, and we made so many families happy, and it had absolutely nothing to do with our website or the products we sell, and that was okay! Our core business is *service*, and that is exactly what we were providing. Plus, I got a chance to tour again, in a way. Not with a rock band, but by putting on these amazing events in cities and towns around the country.

Since then, I've overseen all kinds of projects, suggested by a broad range of employees here, for all sorts of experimental ideas—many of which could turn into whole new businesses for us. All of them are based on service, giving people better experiences in life and business. Like, we had a team put together a better portable toilet to set up at sporting events and concerts, because who doesn't want a better porta-potty experience? They're gross, right? So we created these superclean "porta-parties," with great lighting, mirrors, real sinks, and technology to alleviate the smell.

> *It's a dream job.
> We're innovating,
> exploring,
> experimenting,
> finding ways to
> expand our brand
> and our brand
> of service to the
> world in this
> really genuine,
> entrepreneurial
> way.*

And another team came up with an idea for private work pods we could set up at big business conferences, so attendees could come into the lobby and rent a private mini office space with a work table, just soundproofed enough to block out the noise while they made phone calls and caught up on emails. That's been a big hit. We're trying all sorts of stuff.

Yeah. Brand Aura. That's what I spend my time overseeing these days, and it's awesome. It's a dream job. We're innovating, exploring, experimenting, finding ways to expand our brand and our brand of service to the world in this really genuine, entrepreneurial way that rivals all of the excitement I used to feel when I was out on the road with a rock band. Only here, I do it with a steady paycheck, and I don't have to leave my wife for eight months at a time.

Not a bad gig.

NAVIGATING CHANGES

Derrin Hawkins
Experimental Marketing and Brand Strategy
I once got to pilot a Red Bull Flugtag aircraft (thanks, Tyler!) and dove off a 28-foot ledge into water.

This *was our future.*

Thanks to our core values and the culture we'd fostered, there were stories of employees unleashing their own creative energies all over this company, in all sorts of different ways. They were exceeding expectations—in many cases even their *own* expectations. They were challenging old ways of doing things. They were forming new teams, coming up with new ideas that drove the business forward. The organic nature of employees mentoring each other, promoting from within, the cross-cultivation of ideas across departments—that's where so much of the excitement at Zappos was coming from.

Tony knew this. He saw this and fostered this, long before the Amazon acquisition.

There was just one problem: We weren't all operating under one roof anymore. Since moving from the Bay Area in the early 2000s, the Zappos staff had grown and spread across three buildings on a sprawling campus in Henderson, Nevada. And no matter how many bonding activities we planned or how many All-Hands Meetings we held, there was always a physical separation of various departments within the company because of the layout of the buildings.

The organic nature of employees mentoring each other, promoting from within, the cross-cultivation of ideas across departments— that's where so much of the excitement at Zappos was coming from.

By 2011 Tony had decided it was time to immerse the company in the heart of Las Vegas and to break down the typical barriers that form when organizations become so large that they distance themselves from the community. He could have chosen to move the company just about anywhere. But wherever we moved to had to fall in line with our core values.

Just a few miles from Henderson, one property caught Tony's eye. A property no one wanted: the dilapidated old City Hall building in Downtown Las Vegas. It was a massive concrete structure that was considered ultra-modern when it first opened in 1972. A spot that, up until recently, housed not only a bunch of cramped city offices with low ceilings, but a jail.

I'm pretty sure that when people picture Las Vegas, they mostly envision the Strip. For the past few decades, Vegas's image has been dominated by the Strip's gigantic hotels and casinos. The Bellagio. The Venetian. MGM. Paris. It's the big-money, lit-up, fountain-filled world of entertainment and luxury that was featured in *Ocean's Eleven* and its sequels and a whole bunch of other films since Vegas's rebirth in the "What Happens in Vegas Stays in Vegas" 1990s and early 2000s.

Glamorous is a word that comes to mind. Sexy, even.

Downtown LV is a couple of miles from the Strip, and, in the early 2010s, it might as well have been a million miles away. It's where old-time Vegas flourished half a century ago, in an era that long ago faded. It's where the bright lights of Binion's Gambling Hall and the Golden Nugget still existed but were now drawing in gamblers with far less glamorous budgets to sit in cigarette smoke–filled parlors. In the mid-1990s there was a bold attempt to revitalize downtown's main drag of Fremont Street. The city converted a four-block stretch of that road into a pedestrian walkway, and an entrepreneurial-minded group got together and covered it with a metal canopy that lit up with lights and video projections and gave the area the kind of flash Vegas was famous for. It helped. A little. But overall, outside of the Fremont Street Experience, Downtown LV was a place that most people didn't want to "experience" at all. It was filled with empty lots, empty storefronts, and abandoned buildings. The crime rate was high. It was a place where people didn't dare wander very far from the bright lights after dark. A neighborhood in need of help, and in desperate need of revitalization.

And Tony thought: *Perfect.*

This reminds me of a (possibly apocryphal) story I heard about a shoe company back in the 1800s that sent a couple of their employees to a distant land for . . .

Tony

He put a deal together to lease the City Hall building and remodel it to fit our company culture—raising the ceilings and eliminating walls on most of the floors so everyone could work together and also have a nice view out the windows, while adding a café and outdoor gathering spaces. He also began work behind the scenes, outside of the company, to sink millions of his own dollars into the dreams of a whole bunch of like-minded people to create a Downtown LV revitalization project that would ultimately turn the east end of Fremont Street into a newer, younger, more energetic neighborhood full of bars, restaurants, music venues, and more. The idea was to start buying up some of the abandoned properties downtown and to get the initial groundwork underway for a full-scale revitalization by the time Zappos would be ready to move in.

By early 2012, Tony announced that we were definitely moving—"To Downtown Las Vegas!"

Everybody kind of looked at each other like, *What?*

Some people were excited, some were hesitant, and nearly all of us had some work to do to catch up to Tony's vision. The next year and a half became a whole new adventure in resiliency and navigating change.

It was also a perfect chance for the company's management to figure out how to communicate these sorts of plans to a growing, now 1,400-strong workforce, and to do it with the same sort of love, care, and attention that Zappos service was all about.

Loren Becker
Community Team
Prior to Zappos, I made a living scrubbing barnacles off the bottoms of boats.

Change is hard. I've been here long enough to remember when we first put our core values on paper in 2006. When Tony made it clear that everyone was expected to live by them, there were people who left on their own. And some were given severances to exit because we discovered that their behavior and values didn't align with our values. We only had a few hundred employees then, so it was a blow to see so many go at once. Some people just couldn't understand why they had to be fun and weird now, and why their advancement in the company couldn't just be tied to performance like it might be anywhere else. Like, why did they have to hang out and spend time with their coworkers? So many of the things that have made Zappos a success just felt odd when they were first introduced. It was a big change, and to some people the Core Values seemed silly. Frivolous. Too disruptive. So they left.

We wanted to make this transition easier. We didn't want to say "This is how it is; take it or leave it," the way so many other growing companies might do. We wanted to live up to our first core value, to "Deliver WOW Through Service"—in this case to our own employees. And even though it wasn't my primary role here, I wound up contributing pretty heavily to that effort.

If we'd done a survey at the time of the move announcement, I would say truly half of the employees didn't want to move downtown, so we faced this challenge: How do we convince these people that it's going to be all right?

That wasn't something that could happen overnight. It took time, ultimately requiring us making the move, before people fully got it. But during the transition we opened an office downtown, so at least a few people would start to get a feel for the area. Then we started doing bus tours of the neighborhood, and housing tours, and throwing events downtown, just to get employees to come down and explore and look at Downtown Las Vegas through new eyes.

We did tours of our building while it was under construction, hard-hat tours, so people could see it being put together. We just really wanted to include everyone, from the announcement to the transition, and we found that people had a lot of questions. So we set out to answer them.

I started a magazine as a way to answer employee fears, which was kind of fun and exciting. I knew nothing about publishing. I made the first one on my laptop, in Microsoft Publisher, and stapled it together. I called it the *Downtown Zappos Employee Newsletter*, and it was basically just a resource guide at the beginning: "Hey, here's some information about housing. Here's some information about things to do downtown." People didn't know where to go, what was happening. I included a schedule of events: "Check out this art, check out this concert. Here's the schedule at the Smith Center," a brand-new performing arts center that was opening not too far from our new campus.

I loved that our company would invest in a newsletter like that. And once people saw the first couple of newsletters that I made myself, the investment didn't stop there. The word that came down was "Okay, this is all right. We'll give you more money. Take it out to be printed." So I printed up the next issue in a little square book style, but I was basically doing it all: taking the photos, writing—and I'm not a very good writer. In fact, with the second issue, I challenged the company to find all the grammatical errors. Whoever found them all would get a prize, just to make light of how bad my writing was.

But then a couple of our Zappos copywriters joined the effort, and that really took it to the next level. By the time we were a year into it, we realized that the events schedule and some of the other articles we were writing were useful to the whole downtown community. We changed the name from *Downtown Zappos Employee Newsletter* to *Downtown ZEN*. People picking up an issue might not have known it was a Zappos publication at that point, but that was where the name came from. After having it printed and published, we started putting it in racks all over downtown. I would go to businesses and ask if I could put in a rack, and then once a month I'd do my paper route, coming around on a golf cart dropping off magazines, which was cool in the beginning because I got to meet everyone downtown. The first year we offered free ads to local businesses, just to create some goodwill and get people involved. And by the second year, as construction was wrapping up and we were closer to making the move, we really polished it up. We went to a full-size magazine format, and shortened the name again to the *DT ZEN*. We got a website and an Instagram account and turned it into a real publication. And as it got out into the community a little more, there was less and less content about Zappos moving in and the building construction, and more and more about what was happening in the community.

So not only was it helping our employees get to know DTLV, as Downtown Las Vegas would increasingly become known, but it helped to pull the whole area together and bring a little excitement to all the changes that were happening in the neighborhood.

After we made the move, we actually started selling advertising, and within a few years we were distributing 50,000 copies of *DT ZEN* across the Valley. Print isn't an easy business, and even with the advertising coming in, it didn't really sustain itself for very long. But it was a good run, and we were pretty proud of what we'd put together.

For a little while, *DT ZEN* unexpectedly turned into a whole side business—one that started from the idea that we wanted to make this move downtown and we actually wanted our employees to feel good about it. It came from a point of service. And it served the employees well. I think that one effort made a real difference. And just as the magazine itself morphed from being something just about employees to being something that integrated into the community, a lot of the doubtful Zappos employees eventually morphed into seeing the upside to making the move, and how helping to create a new downtown community would be fun and hopefully good for all of us.

Jeanne Markel
Technical Advisor to CEO Tony Hsieh
I have a weird ability to recognize celebrity voices from TV and radio commercials, even obscure actors I haven't heard in years.

I started way back in early 2006, right before the Core Values were put on paper, and my background has always been in footwear. I was previously a footwear buyer and then general manager. I'm a shoe dog at heart, spending thirty years in that industry. And I came here and I took a step back to start as a buyer, which was a great experience because it was a way to learn not only the Zappos systems but the Zappos culture.

I stayed in footwear here for my first six or seven years, as director of teams, buying mostly casual brands. I was comfortable. I was doing what I knew how to do.

I think "comfortable" is the word that applied to where our offices were as well. I've lived and been in the same house twenty-plus years, in the suburbs, and I really liked where the campus was, not just the convenience of the location but because it was safe and wonderful and familiar.

So when Tony first mentioned, "Hey, we're moving the campus downtown," I admittedly was with the group that thought, *Wow, we're moving to that kind of sketchy, scary place where no one ever goes?*

This was clearly going to push me out of my comfort zone. And it wasn't long after the announcement happened that I got pushed *way* out of my comfort zone for a second time.

Fred Mossler, one of our top executives, who had worked at Nordstrom the same time I did, called me into a room. It was about a five-minute conversation in which he literally said, "Hey, there are a lot of things happening downtown. We kind of need someone to help manage it. Your name's come up. I didn't think of you. I'm not sure it's in your wheelhouse. I'm not sure you're going to like it, but do you want to take this role on and leave this thing that you really enjoy doing?" And I felt like, "Wow, Fred, you have *so* oversold me. I mean, clearly I am the right person for this job!"

For those of you who have not experienced Jeanne's attempts at sarcasm, I highly recommend experiencing it in person. I would give it 5 out of 5 stars on most days.

TONY

But there it was: the opportunity to leave Zappos to join DTP Companies, a separate organization founded by Tony to help revitalize Downtown Las Vegas alongside the effort to move the entire company to the former City Hall property. I wouldn't be working with my team of buyers or the brands I knew and loved, but I would be working closely with Tony and with Fred, and with some of the folks invested in the downtown ecosystem, both within Zappos and with community folks outside the company. There was something exciting about all of that. The whole purpose was to get us as a company to embrace and drive change, and after I said "Yes," I started to really see Tony's vision in action. It was pushing us all outside our comfort zones on purpose. It would be a work in progress—but how exciting and different, and how cool to play whatever part you get to play in being a part of it?

It wasn't going to be easy, but I could see how we might be better for it on the other side.

At the time, that's the way the job change felt, too. It felt scary to me at the time—I was leaving my team. I realize now that I was being a bit dramatic, caught up in emotions. But after a little while I realized I wasn't *really* leaving Zappos, and I would still be interacting with a lot of the same people, plus I'd get to learn a lot of new things.

So I did it. I left and did that for about eleven months.

The way we described Downtown Las Vegas before we moved almost sounds like it was the Wild West or something. And it really was a whole different atmosphere. We'd come downtown and I'd shadow Tony and Fred in their meetings all day, which generally started painfully early, often at seven in the morning, and ran until eleven at night.

> When you embrace change, and drive it, you realize it's an opportunity. You learn from it. You grow from it.

And because of the fact that there wasn't a lot of infrastructure in the downtown ecosystem at the time, and there weren't a lot of bars and restaurants open, we would meet in The Beat coffee shop and have meetings on the hour all day. It was super, super interesting— I think on just day two we had lunch with the mayor! And I would meet a lot of new people—not just high-profile but really interesting businesspeople, community members, guests from out of town—and I realized, "Wow, I would never have had access to meeting such a diverse group in my old job!"

Getting out of my comfort zone turned out to be a really good thing for me. And getting the company out of its comfort zone was going to be good for Zappos, too. The more the plans came together, the more I saw it. And the more other employees began to see it, too, through the tours, and the pieces they read in *DT ZEN*, and the interactions they had with those of us who were already working downtown and seeing all the changes firsthand.

After Zappos made the move, I was offered the chance to come back as a "technical adviser," which is an Amazon title. I'm not "technical" at all, but I'm in a kind of chief-of-staff advisory role with Tony. It's interesting. I've made a lot of changes and moved into different roles in the last few years. It was scary at first to leave my merchandising role and step out of that box, if you will. But I'm happy I did that.

There's a reason why one of our core values is "Embrace and Drive Change." There's a reason we focus on "Growth and Learning."

When change just happens to you, it's scary. It's uncomfortable. The very thought of being pushed out of the comfort zone drives some people away.

But when you embrace change, and drive it, you realize it's an opportunity. You learn from it. You grow from it.

And when you look at it from that perspective, change is *good*.

Kelly Smith
Experimental Marketing and Brand Strategy
I'm currently learning drums as my seventh instrument! Eighth if you include kazoo. ;)

One of the most frequent comments we get from visitors to our Downtown Las Vegas campus today is "WOW. Your employees all seem so happy!"

Despite so many of us putting up a fight and complaining about the move, the reality is that having us all under the same roof helped us all feel more connected. And when you feel connected, you bring that mindset to everything you do.

Moving to DTLV allowed all of our various departments to work more closely together, and it also helped us to work more closely in our community. Downtown LV quickly became an extended part of our campus and family. Meetings and events started happening in various restaurants, bars, and coffee shops in the downtown area. Some of our employees moved into a newly refurbished old downtown casino/hotel building, just steps from campus. The result of all of that is a closer-knit community where work and life seamlessly interact.

In these days of business parks and urban sprawl, our downtown campus feels less isolated from the rest of "life," and there's something really great about that. I've heard Tony liken it to a city college campus, like NYU in New York City, where the average person can't really see where the campus starts or ends. It's simply a part of the city, and the students are a part of the broader community and neighborhood. The school adds vibrancy to the community, and the community adds vibrancy to the school.

I guess what I'm getting at is this: The move worked. Putting everybody under one roof in the downtown setting increased the sort of random interactions and discussions that unleash creativity when so many creative, driven, service-minded people cross paths every day—in the café, in the elevator bank, at local restaurants, at bars after work, or simply in the plaza just outside the lobby, where we all come and go, and where we hold so many community-oriented events.

I've been skateboarding since I was eleven years old. It's kind of been a way of life. Back in 2008, I had been out of high school for about a year and I was aiming to go pro. I was sponsored by Emerica Footwear, which happens to be one of the vendors at Zappos. My rep at the time was also the rep for Zappos, and he said, "Hey, buddy, I've got to go to Zappos; you should come with me." I didn't know what Zappos was, but I was like, "Sure, I'll go with you." We were planning to make a drive to California right after that, so it just made sense to tag along.

I'll never forget when we walked into the lobby—this was at Zappos' Henderson headquarters before they had moved downtown—and there were people playing Dance Dance Revolution right when I walked in. It was like, "Okay, this is . . . I don't know what's going on right here, but this seems cool!" And all of a sudden somebody came up to me and said, "Hey, we're giving out backpacks today. Here you go!" I didn't even say hi yet and they were handing me stuff. I was like, "All right. I like this place!"

The rep I was with had a meeting to go to, so he said, "I've got to run to this office, so I'll see you in like an hour." He just left me on campus, so I went wandering around, not really knowing what this place was or what anybody did for work, but I could tell everybody was smiling and really enjoying what they were doing. People were talking to each other, and joking around, and it just seemed like the camaraderie was really fun.

When we left, I called up my buddy Gonzo and said, "Man, we should both apply to Zappos and get a job there. It's sweet!"

After I got back from California, I wound up applying to the Hard Rock Café instead. It just seemed like it would be a cool place to work, too. But my buddy Gonzo took my advice and applied at Zappos, and he landed a job there. I ended up working at the Hard Rock Café as a host for a long time, but I was still a sponsored skater, and I was doing well. I was getting ready to move to California to pursue skateboarding full time. I had already quit Hard Rock and everything, and then, two days before my move, I blew out my left knee. It was bad. I needed surgeries. My whole dream just came to a halt. Right then and there, all of my sponsorships got cut.

I went into surgery and shortly ran out of money. I had to move to Texas to live with my auntie, offering to help her around the house and do odds and ends if she paid me a little bit while I healed. I really didn't know what I was going to do with my life. I had pinned all my dreams on a skateboarding career.

I forget how many months went by, but after a while, I heard from Gonzo. "Hey, did you still want to work at Zappos?" he asked me, and I was like, "Yeah, dude. Help me. I'll do anything right now."

Gonzo helped me get my foot in the door, and I started working the phones at Zappos. It was awesome, just talking to people and making people happy all day. It took me a while to adjust, actually. I kept putting people on hold and asking, "Can I really give them these shoes for free? Can I really upgrade their shipping? Are you sure I should say yes to this return?" I kept thinking I'd get in trouble for doing too much, you know? But I got with the program soon enough, and then I was promoted to the team that gives all our WOW gifts that we send to our customers based on those awesome connections, so cookies and flowers and all that good jazz. I came to love this place, just like everyone else here. But my skateboarding career just faded into the background. I was off it for over a year, and, even when I was able to skate again, I knew I couldn't take it to the next level. I had to let that dream fade.

Still, I hoped I could get involved in some way with the skateboarding world. I had conversations with our buyers here, thinking I might be able to take my career in that direction—picking out the shoes and clothes and things that skateboarders would like so we could sell it. But the more I learned about what it entailed, I realized that wasn't the path I wanted to take.

Another opportunity to integrate my skateboarding knowledge into my work here came up pretty quickly, though. Zappos threw a skateboarding event on Fremont Street in Downtown Las Vegas, and I raised my hand to help. There wasn't much of a budget that first year. They built a ramp that was only about waist high. I remember walking up to it and thinking, "This is not going to be good." I was glad we were trying at least, because Zappos wasn't really known in the skateboarding world as a go-to place. As a skateboarder, I know I wasn't going to Zappos to buy my stuff, but I was like, "We have the venue to make it happen. We've just got to let people know they can buy their gear through us!" But that first event was definitely kind of lame. There wasn't a whole lot of WOW there.

I really wanted to do something awesome, and I let the events team know it. I gave my input, and they listened, and every year those events got better.

But it wasn't until we moved the whole company to the Downtown LV campus that it really hit me: There's a big ol' stair set outside, and metal rails, and this awesome plaza. I had looked at this thing before we even moved here and wished I could've skated here. But then it was off limits. It was City Hall. There were police present 24/7. And even after Zappos took over the space, there were security guards around the perimeter. It was still off limits. But from a skateboarder's standpoint, I was like, "We've got to skate this thing. I don't know how or when it's going to happen, but it's got to happen!"

That's when I got the idea: We should do a skating event here. Quit shutting down Fremont Street. Quit building all these big ol' ramps. "I promise you," I told the team in charge of the event, "if you have the best skateboarders come here and jump down the stairs, magic will happen."

Lo and behold, the team listened to me. They told me to go for it. We set up this skateboarding event on campus, and I think to this day it's probably one of the biggest events that we've ever had. There were 4,000 people clogged in the plaza! We had money to give out for the best tricks, and one after another these skaters got up there and started jumping those steps, and the craziest tricks started happening. It was magic. It was totally unscripted. It wasn't like we had an emcee saying, "And next up is so-and-so from Omaha doing a 360"—nothing. I told them, "Nah, nah, just let the magic happen. Put skaters in this environment, and magic will happen." And it did.

Prior to this event, I had asked our legal and risk teams if we could turn our six-story parking garage into a giant playground for skateboarders on weekends, free to the skateboarding community. I was expeditiously told no ("What if a skateboarder accidentally jumps over one of the walls on the upper floors?"), so I was super excited to see Jovahn's event in person. You can check out some of the videos from it here: https://www.zappos.com/about/good-times-and-fire-rhymes.

How amazing was that? At some other company, the higher-ups might put people in a boardroom or run a focus group to try to figure out how to put on the coolest skateboarding event, and I can guarantee you what they'd come up with wouldn't be cool. This was *cool*. It was so rewarding to see it all come together, and to see Zappos finally look as cool as it ought to look in the eyes of the skating world. I'm just so proud of what happened that day and the teamwork that went into making it happen.

And now, I've got dreams of launching a skate park in Downtown Las Vegas. A Zappos-branded skate park. That's a lifelong dream—to have a place like that right here in the downtown area—and I'm pretty sure we're going to make it happen. Why not? And then we can have our events at the Zappos skate park every year.

I'm just so thankful to work at a place that values who I am and what I bring to the table. And it goes beyond the skateboarding, too. That's just a once-a-year thing.

What's even better is in June 2016, we went on a team-building excursion and I made a fun little video for my birthday that day. I edited it and turned it around superfast, giving it to Tyler Williams, who heads up the Brand Aura team. And Tyler was like, "Yo, man, do you make these? Like, is this something you do on the regular?" I'd learned to do some video stuff to document my skateboarding as a teenager, but I told him I did it just for funsies, nothing serious.

"We need stories for Zappos to crank out at this type of speed, so I'm willing to try and come up with some role that fits for you in Brand Aura," he said. Next thing I knew, I joined the Brand Aura team and became a content publisher for our blogs platform. I started shooting video around the company, looking for great stories to tell. And I remember those first few months asking Tyler, "What stories? What do you want me to go get?" and he was like, "Just go get stories. Don't ask me; just go get them." So that was what I did, and I've been doing blogs for a couple of years now, and our readership has been climbing. My storytelling skills are getting much better, too. So I'm very, very excited about that.

Everything happens for a reason. The main difference here at Zappos is that people notice. When things happen, they matter. The reasons become part of what we do. Our passions become our focus, and then we have the backing to make those passions real. And that just ups the experience for everyone.

John Krikorian
Customer Loyalty Team

The "backing" here is about so much more than business. There's a feeling of camaraderie. The fact that we're all under the same roof and see each other every day, the way people genuinely care about each other—even with 1,500 people or whatever our staff has grown to these days, it feels like we're all part of a family. And that's not an exaggeration. I genuinely feel like no matter what was to befall me, I'd be fine because of the people I work with.

I remember a few years ago, during wintertime, right before Christmas, my central air and heat went out. It was a roof unit and it was going to cost me nearly $8,000 to replace it. I didn't have the money out of pocket to cover that big of an expense that year, and before I even had time to consider financing options, my boss set up a GoFundMe to help cover the expense, and a bunch of my coworkers contributed to the fund. Even my old boss who didn't work here anymore gave a huge amount of money. It was just cool. I was able to get the unit replaced and still buy nice Christmas presents for my kids.

I feel like no matter what happened, I would be okay. I've got a 1,500-person support system.

Jamie Naughton
Chief of Staff

I have an intense sense of smell. It's both a blessing and a curse.

People hear these stories of employees supporting each other, and the smiles at the office, and I think they get some things wrong about us. Like, in the past people have joked that we're some kind of a workplace "cult" or something, and it just couldn't be further from the truth. We hire for values, but the way those values play out, the way they're expressed—no one looks or acts the same here. As you meet more and more Zappos employees you realize each one of us is so different. We bring different strengths to the table, and we express the Core Values in varying degrees. But when the hiring process goes well, and so many of us come together with the same values, you really wind up liking the people you work with—even if they're really, really different from you.

We don't expect everyone to be smiling all the time. That's not a rule or something. We just create a fun atmosphere and work environment for our employees at this campus. We embrace diversity. We want our employees to bring their whole selves to work, and being human means that you have ups and downs. And sometimes your downs affect your work, and sometimes your ups affect your work. If you're getting married, maybe your focus isn't so much on the day-to-day at the office. We get it. Or maybe someone in your life just passed away and now your focus is somewhere else. I can't imagine working for a company that didn't understand that.

In the fourteen years I've been with Zappos—it's going to sound like I'm a catastrophe—I've had a house fire, two miscarriages, three babies, a divorce, a marriage, and the grief of my mom passing away last year. And every time, Zappos has been so key to my healing or my celebrating the stuff that's happening in my life. I have a tribe here. We all have a tribe. A family. Whatever you want to call it.

When my mom passed away, I found out at like eight o'clock at night, and within an hour there were three coworkers at my house. The next day, there were ten. But that's just me. I want to be surrounded by people in times of need, and all the time, really. I know an employee whose mom passed away recently, and she's the opposite. She said, "I love you. Text me as much as you want. But please don't come around." I respect that. We all do. We respect people's needs *and* their boundaries here, in every way we can.

All of that makes us stronger as a company. Not weaker. Stronger. In every way.

I can do my work better when I don't feel like I'm sacrificing my family to be here. I don't get bitter that Zappos is taking so much of my time away from my family because when my family starts needing more from me, Zappos will get a little less of me for a while. And when Zappos needs more of me, my family will get a little less for a while. And it doesn't take a lot of bending over backward and additional stress to manage that give and take, because the company takes a human approach to everything we do. And, as I hope so many of our examples have shown, the payoff for that is the longevity we have. The retention we have. The opportunities we have to see our employees grow into new roles, because they love working here and want to give their all to a company that does its best to give its all to them.

SHARING VALUES

Jeff Espersen
Head of Merchandising
I love doing DIY projects. I remodeled my master bath, kitchen, outdoor fireplace, and barbecue island.

Clearly, we hire people who are not only passionate about what they do but also ethical, trustworthy, nice, and so on. And we all work together in a way that supports those traits and those values. That can't be said about some other workplaces. I've had previous jobs where I've walked by people and said "hi" to them, and they just keep walking. It's like, "Really? Come on. It's not that hard."

By hiring people who see and know the difference between those two types of environments, we wind up with a lot of really, really hard-working folks who are pretty passionate about making this company successful. Everybody plays a part, and I like to think that everybody feels valued for playing their part.

But there's something else that comes with that: When we're secure in who we are and what we do, which is first and foremost WOWing through service, we don't have to spend a lot of time worrying about what our competitors are doing. We just don't. Instead, we're free to worry about what *we're* doing.

Where a lot of companies go wrong, I think, is when they start spending more time worried about what their competitors are doing than they spend focused on themselves. We stay aware of what's going on in the marketplace, of course. That's just part of business. It never makes sense to put on blinders. But when it comes to adjusting to new challenges and growing our business, our culture here allows us to focus on what *we* can do better, knowing that whatever we do better will automatically differentiate us from our competitors—because we're not trying to "be like them."

And the funny thing is that turning inward and focusing on what we're doing well and what we can do better isn't a selfish thing. Not at all. In fact, we have a long history here of sharing what we learn with others, including our competitors.

In that respect, I guess you could say we're an open book. After all: We've written this book that you've opened!

Christa Foley
Head of Brand Vision, Head of Talent Acquisition, and Head of External Culture Training

My favorite drink is a vodka martini, straight up, blue cheese olives . . . but the key is it needs to be pornographically dirty!

For the record, I introduced both vodka martinis and blue cheese olives to Christa's world, although I prefer my martinis extra clean and super dry. In other words, no vermouth. In other words, just straight, chilled vodka. By the way, it's also really hard to find good blue cheese olives. The ones at Ruth's Chris Steakhouse are delicious. I always order extra blue cheese olives anytime I go there.

Long before we decided to write this book, and long before we came up with the title for it, we opened a branch of Zappos called Zappos Insights just to share the philosophies you're now reading about with the world.

To the public, we offer tours of our Downtown LV campus. But to corporate America we offer three-day Culture Camps, a School of WOW, one-on-one Q&A sessions with Zappos department specialists, Zappos keynote speakers, and more. And over the years, all sorts of corporations have taken us up on those offers.

Holding on to company secrets is one thing. Holding on to company philosophies and practices that we firmly believe could make the world a better place just seems wrong. So we share what we know—which hopefully pushes other organizations (even our "competitors") forward, which in turn pushes us to keep innovating and moving forward ourselves.

It's a pretty wild cycle of growth and knowledge that comes when you invite other companies into your space and basically open up a school to share your knowledge rather than hide it from the world. It sort of shifts the traditional corporate paradigm on its head, doesn't it? And we've never regretted sharing any of the Insights we've shared.

> It also happens to align with our purpose statement: to inspire the world by showing it's possible to simultaneously deliver happiness to customers, employees, community, vendors, and shareholders in a long-term, sustainable way.

I think most of us grew up with an achievement mindset. And Zappos really pushes a *growth* mindset. We're fostering the growth of our own people, and other people, and other companies, and we truly want to inspire the world to create a better way to work, and to be.

> *I would much rather work at a place where selling a product comes second to delivering service, and growing as a person is just as important as, if not more important than, growing the numbers.*

I can honestly say that I think I'm a better person, a *happier* person, for working here. I have a teenage son. I'm a single mom. And I think he has a better life and is happier and more well-adjusted because of my working here. And so much of that comes back to the basic concept of feeling like what you're doing is contributing to something bigger than just trying to make money, you know? I had eight years in the traditional corporate world before I came here, and I worked with some great people and the companies I worked for had some great qualities. But in the end, there were so many things that just felt like a transaction, "just business." And whenever that phrase is brought up, "It's just business," doesn't it just suck the life out of the room? It's not a good feeling. I would much rather work at a place where selling a product comes second to delivering service, and growing as a person is just as important as, if not more important than, growing the numbers.

Growth isn't easy. When Tony pushed me to move from recruiting into Zappos Insights, it was a really hard transition for me. I'd been in recruiting for fifteen years. I didn't know anything about B2B (business-to-business), especially with an educational focus. But it's been seven years since I moved to Zappos Insights, and I love it! (Fun note: I also just got the chance to help lead the recruiting team again, so it's all come full circle. ☺)

The lesson it taught me, which I hope I'm passing along to my son, is that if you're making a tough decision and your reason to say "no" is simply because it makes you uncomfortable, or you're unsure that you can slam-dunk it, that's not a good reason *not* to do it.

So tell me again why you won't go onstage for our All Hands Meetings, Christa? ☺

That lesson applies in business as much as it applies to any individual's life.

Those lessons have impacted my life for sure, along with thinking about all of our core values and thinking about my *personal* values. I hadn't given them much consideration before I came here. I'm not sure if most people think about their morals in such concrete terms.

But it all matters. It all makes life at work and at home a little better, maybe a lot better, when you stand on a firm foundation.

It's not always perfect, of course. Just because you share common values doesn't mean you don't disagree. A relationship isn't all rainbows and sunshine all the time, and this type of workplace is all about relationships. A family isn't all easy, either. There are struggles. And the bigger our Zappos family gets, the more struggles there are going to be. But the difference, I think, is that no matter what happens, we work together. We may disagree, but we work through it, because we all want to succeed. We all want this *company* to succeed. And we really do care about each other, and our customers, and everyone we work with—both inside and outside this building.

John Krikorian
Customer Loyalty Team
I own a pig named Fig.

I just want to mention our Holiday Helper program again, because it really gets to the heart of what we experienced through the move downtown, and through all of the remarkable and frankly scary changes that would start to unfold after we made that move. And what it reminds all of us is that we're all in this together. Zappos isn't a company of "them" and "us," the higher-ups and the lower workers. The top of the pyramid versus the bottom. None of that. And we get reminded of that every year.

When I started in 2009, we were constantly hiring. We simply didn't have enough people to deal with our call volume. During our most important time of the year, we needed as much help as possible. We used to require everybody outside of CLT to assist customers during the busiest season, typically Black Friday through the end of January or something like that.

Over the years, it's evolved a little bit because we don't really *need* the help anymore. We have enough staff to work the phones, and we have the ability to hire seasonal help when we have big call volume. But Tony and the leadership have always believed that it's an important enough part of our tradition here to keep alive. And I agree.

It's a reminder that no matter what your job is in the company, what you do has an impact on the customer. It's important for people to connect with customers and remember what firsthand customer service feels like.

At the same time, it drives empathy for CLT, because sometimes our hourly folks on the phones can feel isolated from the rest of the company. Zappos works hard to not make them feel that way, but seeing people from all over Zappos sitting next to you on the phones during Christmas hours is one surefire way to eliminate that feeling.

It also helps drive tech innovation for us. When someone from tech is working the phones during the holidays and dealing with customer issues directly, and they notice something in the system is slow or difficult or clunky, they're inspired to change and improve it. As an example, we had one advanced type of exchange that used to be a multistep process in our system.

An "advanced exchange" has been a fun little secret thing we do for anyone that calls in and wants to process an exchange (usually the same style, just for a different size). We will send the replacement pair of shoes out to the customer during the phone call before we've received the original pair back. Customers are WOWed because we trust them.

Tony

One of our developers encountered that issue firsthand and sat down the very next day to write some code that changed that process to a single button. One button and all the bells would go off and it would do everything for you. Amazing.

But the best part of it all is truly sending that signal to our whole company, year after year, that we're all in this together. Tony always, every year, signs up to work the phones on some of our biggest call-volume days. For example, December 26, the day after Christmas, is when everybody under the sun calls with exchanges, returns, gift certificates they received in their stockings, and so much more.

It's just really cool to see him there, right alongside everybody else.

I remember way back when I was a helper in CLT, and Tony was up there and he needed help processing a refund or something. I was like, "This is so weird. I'm assisting my CEO with helping a customer!"

I asked him then, "How do you introduce yourself on the phone? Do you say anything?"

He said, "I was, for a little bit, saying, 'Hey, this is Tony the CEO!' but people would just be like, 'Hey, Tony, I need a new pair of shoes.' They didn't really care all that much. So I stopped. I just introduce myself like anyone else here."

Keeping up this tradition is not something that *has* to happen. But it keeps people grounded and connected to what everybody's here for, and to the driving force of the company.

Jeanne Markel
Technical Advisor to CEO Tony Hsieh

This year my husband and I decided to visit all thirty MLB ballparks and a winery in every state. So far, we are seven out of thirty on the ballparks, and only five out of fifty on wineries—so we have a ways to go!

Knowing we all work the phones every year, knowing we made the transition to Downtown LV together—it all adds up to making it seem like we can make *any* transition together. It amplifies the feeling of family in this company, and I feel that I can't say this without it being cheesy, but, for me, this *is* my family. Like, *literally*. (My actual family at home would just laugh and say, "Yup! They're her family all right," because they're an extended part of the Zappos family, too.) The things that we do together and the way we interact with each other—I just don't think that exists elsewhere. And I wish it did.

After working here for so long, and seeing what we've been through and where we're headed, I truly have the mindset that if we get the right people on the bus, this bus full of people is going to figure it out. No matter what happens. No matter what road-blocks or potholes we hit, we're going to work together to figure out the best way to get through it, or over it, or around it.

I can't stress how important that mindset has become to this company.

By the time we settled into our new digs in Downtown Las Vegas, I think many of us gained the confidence to know that even when we're doing hard things, things that haven't been done before, this is the group that we want to be with, no matter what.

Whatever we need to do, however we need to support each other, however we need to adapt or change to keep moving forward, we know this group can do it.

DRIVING CHANGE

Tony Hsieh
CEO
I love making random soups out of leftovers.

FYI, the content in "my" section you're about to read was based on Mark's interviews with me but actually ghostwritten by Mark. Although I might not have used these exact words (like "management" or "leaders"), the content is accurate and represents my point of view. But these "thought bubbles," such as the one you're reading now, are all written by me. Welcome to the behind-the-scenes world of book publishing. ☺

Someone from the traditional business world might have looked at Zappos as we headed into 2014 and said, "Great! You're all under one roof, you've settled into your new partnership, you've got a great thing going here! Just keep doing what you're doing. Don't rock the boat. Find new ways to dig more profits out of this awesome business you've already built and you'll be *golden*."

That was not a chance I was willing to take, plus I would probably be bored if we were just doing the same thing forever.

The average life span of an S&P 500 company is around fifteen years. We were *there*. If we coasted now, if we took the typical road of "efficiency" and "cutbacks" and staying in our comfort zone, we knew our decline would eventually come, since the default future for companies is death. (In general, the research has shown that companies do not stand the test of time.) Not to mention, if there was a major shift in the market-place that drove customers away from online sales, or some other unexpected change happened that we couldn't predict—that being the nature of unexpected change—who knows what might happen?

It wasn't the time to coast. It was time for us to get ahead of the curve. It was time to double down on our core value of "Embrace and Drive Change," in order to make Zappos more resilient.

It was time to take what we'd accomplished as a company so far and find new ways to take it to the next level, on our own unique terms.

To me, that meant making changes in management structure. Not by hiring and firing. Not changing up the team. But implementing a new managerial structure that would move myself and our entire typical, top-down hierarchical managerial structure out of the way—to allow for the progress, innovation, and resiliency that we'd planted firmly in the roots of this company to grow and flourish.

Imagine a greenhouse full of plants, and imagine each plant represents a single employee.

At a typical company, the CEO might be viewed as the biggest, strongest, maybe the most charismatic plant that all of the other plants strive to one day become. That's not how I've ever viewed myself or my role as CEO.

In other companies, the CEO might be the chief gardener at the greenhouse, the one who micromanages every plant's well-being by digging his or her hands into the soil and measuring the acidity of the water supply. (Is that something gardeners do? I'm not sure. I've never gardened before.) Anyway, that's not how I view myself, either.

When I think of my role here at Zappos, I think of my role more as being like the architect of the greenhouse, where under the right conditions, the plants will flourish and thrive on their own. I want to make sure that everything is built to certain standards and maintained properly so that all of the plants inside will grow and reach their full potential. I might step in to replace a window or adjust the framing now and then, even move us to a new greenhouse if needed, but for the most part I like to stay out of the way—so I don't cast a shadow that slows down the natural growth.

That's pretty much been the theme for me for most of my adult life now.

I used to throw a lot of parties, but I was never the *life* of the party. I was more interested in organizing the flow and seeing what happened when people from different walks of life collided in that environment, encouraged by music, lights, the set-up of the rooms, the locations of the bars, and so on. At the Airstream Park where I live, there are always interesting collisions around the campfire. I remember one Sunday not too long ago, Jewel, the singer-songwriter, happened to be in town. And we had a local beatboxer performing with a local freestyle rapper, and Jewel wound up joining them, and the trio improvised a couple songs together that had never been heard before and will never be heard again in the exact same way.

It was amazing. I never could have made that music happen on my own. It's unlikely that I'm ever going to be a beatboxer, or

> *If even one out of every 100 random collisions results in something creative, something interesting, something positive, something profitable, or something innovative, then the ROI is there.*

a rapper, or Jewel. I can't do what those people can do. Even if I were their manager, I wouldn't necessarily have thought to mix those artists together. But it happened in a completely spontaneous and serendipitous way, and it was awesome.

That sort of randomness can yield results in business, too. That's why I wanted everyone at Zappos under one roof again: just to see what would grow from it. And sure, what comes from those random interactions is sometimes just randomness. But in my experience, if even only one out of every 100 random collisions results in something creative, something interesting, something positive, something profitable, or something innovative, then the ROI is there. And in my experience, the batting average of those random collisions resulting in something positive is usually much higher than 1 in 100.

What's changed for me the most in the last decade is that even the idea of the greenhouse just seems too small. A business at scale shouldn't be so constrained. A greenhouse could still come down in a storm.

So how can a business survive the storms and outlast the pace of change?

The answer, I believe, lies in resiliency. And resiliency is a complex recipe. It calls for creativity, inspiration, humanity, progress built on firm (but flexible) beliefs and solid foundations—the very things that we've tried to foster here at Zappos from the start.

How can a CEO, or traditional managers in general, stay out of the way of progress, creativity, and inspiration when we're all working under a top-down, pyramid-shaped managerial structure that hasn't changed in nearly a hundred years? As companies get bigger, they generally become more bureaucratic, slower moving, and less innovative. It isn't any one person's fault, it's just a function of the size and hierarchical structure of the company.

Why do we do that when we know that the endgame for almost any business under that old managerial style of corporate growth is ultimately to go out of business?

Way back in the early 2000s, it wasn't me or another executive or some focus group but one of the employees in our call center who came up with the perfect phrase to describe what we do here at Zappos: "We're a service company that just happens to sell shoes." That phrase is as accurate today as it was back then—although we sell a lot more than shoes these days. We're a service company first, but the specific products that we sell is something that can and likely will change over time. Twenty, thirty, forty years from now, shoes might be looked at as just those things that we started selling way back when, the same way books are now viewed as just one of the millions of products sold by Amazon. I'm sure there are customers of Virgin Airlines or Virgin Hotel who don't even remember there was ever such a thing as Virgin Records—the brick-and-mortar music stores that went out of business so long ago, or the record label that Richard Branson founded so many decades ago. Virgin as a brand and as a collection of different businesses still exists. It just evolved and grew over time.

Richard Branson has a unique character, as the charismatic founder of Virgin, and so much of the evolution of that company depended on his personal vision. But not every company has a Richard Branson. (In fact, no other company has a Richard Branson.) So is it even possible to think along Bransonian lines in a non-Virgin world?

How do we make our business, *any* business, evolve with the times and last for decades to come? What types of organizations could we model ourselves after? What types of organizations or organisms or systems have a history of outlasting most businesses on Earth?

I've read hundreds of business books and articles, many of which I've shared with our employees through the Zappos library. I've been fortunate enough to spend time with some really interesting CEOs, founders, and researchers of all types since I started asking these questions, too, and I've brought some of them in to speak to our employees. And through all of the research and consideration, the best example I've come up with so far in terms of the type of human organization that is resilient, that scales, and that stands the test of time—and which also happens to be one of the best examples of self-organization that scales—is: the city.

> *The resilient organization we ought to strive to emulate is a city. Cities can thrive and last for hundreds, even thousands, of years. Even while empires and countries around them crumble, great cities survive. They evolve. Constantly. And for the most part, they're self-organized.*

Cities can thrive and last for hundreds, even thousands, of years. Even while empires and countries around them crumble, great cities survive.

Why?

Because they evolve. Constantly. And for the most part, they're self-organized.

The mayor of a city doesn't actually tell its residents what to do or where to live. The mayor doesn't determine whether or not a specific business pops up or how that business is run. In a city, it's okay to have multiple businesses doing the same thing, sometimes many of them in the same neighborhood. It's the opposite of the typical corporate way of thinking, which assumes that any duplication of work is not "efficient" and needs to be "streamlined" to be "more efficient."

There's a price that's paid for all of that efficiency. Any time you try to do something to increase stability or increase efficiencies, both of which are easily measurable (or at least *easier* to measure), it usually comes at the cost of resilience—and resilience is actually what matters in the long term for a company. For any organization.

In the more typical, hierarchical corporate environment, as you become more efficient and better at one thing, it works really well—until it doesn't, when the world changes, competition changes, technology changes, whatever. Without the resiliency, the diversity, the ability to stay nimble as a city does, once-great companies or some of the major record labels and technology firms of the past just got wiped out overnight.

I don't want that for Zappos.

In order to stand the test of time, why not remake Zappos into something that operates more like a city and less like a top-down hierarchy?

That's where my head was as 2014 approached.

I wanted to do more of what we'd done best in this company. Not more in terms of how much product we sold, although, as we'd shown through most of our history, that tends to come automatically when everything else is working. But I wanted Zappos to fulfill its more-human promises. To amplify the importance of and support for our core values. To be the best at customer service and customer experience, for everyone in the equation.

If one of our big goals was to bring our full, whole selves to work, and for our work to more seamlessly integrate into our lives, then how could we do even more of that?

If we'd proven that we had developed a degree of resiliency through the Amazon acquisition and the move to Downtown LV, how could we take this resilient workforce that we'd assembled and push it toward a brighter future? One that would continue to grow no matter what changes might come?

Unfortunately for us, some of those changes were already at our doorstep. Heading into 2014, we were facing headwinds. The marketplace was changing. Our competitors had upped their game. For the first time since the Amazon deal was finalized in 2009, we were looking at the possibility that revenue and profits might be down in the upcoming quarters.

Was the answer to stop thinking long term and just focus on the short-term day-to-day? To start laying off the very employees that made Zappos so strong? To cut corners? To scale back to get our numbers up?

None of those felt right.

We wanted to move forward for the long-term benefit of all of us, which has always been our goal.

So the answer was to make a significant change that would give our employees even more autonomy than they already had. To flip the traditional managerial model on its head and give our employees more power than ever to make unhindered decisions for the sake of the company.

To take away the old managerial structure and put something new in its place.

To move Zappos toward a system of more city-like self-organization.

So in January 2014, we officially took our first steps towards self-organization: we made the shift to Holacracy.

John Bunch
Organizational Systems and Advisor
to CEO Tony Hsieh
*I would wear the same pair of jeans unwashed
for years if it weren't for my wife stealing them
and washing them.*

Tony had been interested in the idea of self-organiza-
tion for a long time, and Holacracy was the vehicle that at the
time had the best codified system for helping an organization
get there.

The ideas for this big change sprung from this sense that as we
grew, as we transitioned from a small start-up to a medium-sized
enterprise, things we used to be able to get done quickly weren't
so quick anymore, and we were just not able to innovate or evolve
as fast as we wanted to.

Stepping back to reflect on that, it was an obvious outcome,
one that happens to most organizations.

There's a book that Tony really tuned in to called *Triumph of
the City* by Edward Glaeser, and it's based on all of this research
showing how cities are these amazing engines of society. And
we're at a tipping point now where more people are living in
cities than rural areas for the first time in history.

> *Approximately more than 50 percent of all
> humans now live in cities. Within our lifetime, that
> number will jump to 75 percent.*

Why? Because cities, as the book posits, "Make Us Richer,
Smarter, Greener, Healthier, and Happier." And part of the reason
for that is what's born out in the research: Every time the size of

a city doubles, innovation and productivity per resident increases by 15 percent. There's an exponentiality to cities. And the exact opposite is true for most organizations, especially business organizations: Every time the size of an organization doubles, productivity tends to go way down.

So Tony got to thinking, "How can we think of ourselves more like a city, or a complex adaptive system," which is what a city is, "and less like a traditional business organization?"

> *Every time the size of a city doubles, innovation and productivity per resident increases by 15 percent . . . Every time the size of an organization doubles, productivity tends to go way down.*

One of the biggest components of that is this concept of self-organization: a system in which there are rules but no rulers. There's a set of rules that the game operates under, just like in a city. There are governments that make laws and regulations, but there are no "rulers"—no one person directing you what to do and how to do it.

In a lot of organizations, the managerial structure is top-down. Command and control. You take marching orders from your manager, and the manager has the ability and authority to override any decision you might make.

Holacracy provides a framework to break through that.

For a deep dive into the origins of Holacracy, I recommend picking up the book: Holacracy: The New Management System for a Rapidly Changing World *by Brian J. Robertson.*

Tony

To put it in simple terms, Holacracy is a vehicle, a set of guidelines and structures, that helps to push an organization toward self-organization.

One example of what sets self-organization apart is that, in a traditional company, one person is on *one* team doing *one* essential job function. Self-organization breaks that by allowing one person to be on *multiple* teams, or in *multiple* "circles," as they're called (there's a whole language built around Holacracy's organizational framework). That means one person can work on different efforts throughout the organization.

Self-organization is a system in which there are rules but no rulers.

Just that one change, in and of itself, setting all other mechanics aside, is fairly revolutionary and allows for a lot of interesting and novel ideas to emerge. It can help eliminate siloing. And it provides the opportunity for employees to start new circles, too, to pursue ideas that pull people into that new circle from across the organization as needed.

The "boss" of any one of those circles is called the "lead link." But those bosses aren't traditional bosses, because self-organization also calls for integrative decision-making—basically, bringing the concept of democracy to the corporate structure through a system of governance.

The lead link of any circle can pretty much make any decision that person wants, including restructuring, moving things around, assigning tasks. And that might sound just like being a "manager," but it's not, because the way all things are handled in a self-organized system looks a little bit different. Each employee is given a voice, so that they can safely bring up tensions and process them through a system of checks and balances. Each circle has not just a lead link but a rep link as well, who can process tensions on behalf of the circle up to the super circle (the next layer) when necessary. Rep links are voted into position for an allotted amount of time and that role gets rotated on a timetable determined by the circle. Lead links can also delegate their typical managerial responsibilities, such as budgetary and planning responsibilities, out to the team so that he or she has more time to actually be *part* of the team.

This system of governance is meant to put policies and regulations in place as needed and to also build a structure for the circle, including creating new roles, removing or modifying those roles, adjusting a circle's purpose, and adding/removing accountabilities for various roles.

In a traditional organization, the manager would say, "We've got a new policy everybody needs to abide by. Here it is." But with self-organization, there's a process by which anybody can propose a policy, and then follow a process to integrate other perspectives and/or objections to the policy before it's put into place. In that way, you're able to make changes to regulations without there being a single person in charge of making that regulation. That's at the core of governance.

For example, say your circle is running a little grocery store that carries every vegetable but no fruit. Customers come in expressing interest in buying bananas. Any member of the circle can say, "I think we should create a new role for someone to purchase bananas so we can start selling them." The proposal is then run by everyone else to ask questions, such as "Will this cause harm or move us backward in any way?" Someone might say, "Yes, it might cost a lot of money if they don't sell." That objection is then looked at for what it is: "Is that an anticipated fear? Or an actual result? And even if that's the case, how much would it cost? Is it safe enough to try?" If the answer leans toward "Well, I guess it's safe enough to try," then the banana idea is done and adopted.

The goal of that isn't to slow things down. It's to *discourage* putting policies in place that will slow things down unintentionally—to think through policies and get feedback on them, from everyone who will be affected by them, *before* they are put into place.

Because any circle member can surface a tension and make a proposal at any time, it also truly gives employees autonomy to move their team and, ultimately, the business forward. Instead of waiting for the executives to make huge decisions that slowly trickle from the top down, the rest of the company can make improvements and changes at *any* given time to constantly evolve the company. In the end, it actually is faster.

When it comes to structuring the work, there are circles, roles, and accountabilities, and all of that goes through a governance process as well. It's a way to allow decisions and structures to be made without relying on one person to be the filter/decider of all things. And there's a second process called the "tactical process," which uses efficient, fast-paced meetings to keep the circle moving through projects and make sure things remain in motion, so nothing gets stuck.

Just to be clear, most decisions don't have to go up the governance chain. The circles are free to do what they do, independently. They're given more power and control, which automatically gives them greater ability to be nimble and change direction as needed.

One of the big goals of self-organization is to keep the regulatory layer as lean as possible.

In some other organizations you have to ask for permission before doing pretty much anything outside of your normal day-to-day job function. The default with self-organization is the opposite. Unless there is a specific policy and/or restriction on it, you can do whatever you think is in the best interest of your circle or role.

Basic decisions don't go through any layers of governance, which is really more of a backup system. Something that's "tension driven." It's there to help, and, in some cases, tensions can go all the way to the top, to the General Company

Circle (GCC), which involves Tony and the company's top decision-makers. But overall, governance tries to stay away from making policies based on anticipated harm. To over-simplify it, governance is really only there to add regulation when something goes wrong, when we don't want that wrong thing repeated.

After a trial run in a small test group in 2013, Tony launched the new system of self-organization all at once in January 2014, and, to be honest, there was a bit of chaos at first. Everyone tried to do what the rollout said they had to do, but there were a lot of rules and processes to the circles and governance that were really confusing. Almost no one got it right away.

Looking back, I would say there are probably lighter-weight ways to get a lot of the benefits of self-organization without the cumbersome launch. But at the end of the day, Holacracy is just a platform, and there are lots of things that have to be built on that platform to move toward true self-organization.

Maybe one way to look at this is as a pendulum. In a traditional hierarchy, the pendulum swings toward the control side: Everybody lives on a team and is very clear on what to do, but there's not a lot of autonomy. As we jumped into self-organization, people very quickly got interested in creating circles and building groups around new ideas, with some great innovation and benefits coming out of that, as you'll see in Part III of the book. But we also had circles that sprang up that just didn't fit the Zappos ethos and mission. People thought they were doing what's right. We didn't have great feedback loops in place to tell us whether what they were doing was truly providing any value to Zappos in a way that made sense for our business.

In hindsight, the pendulum swung a little too quickly from control to freedom—faster than we were ready to handle. We saw some of our core business metrics start to take a hit because of that. Customer response time from CLT groups slowed down. We realized there was a problem there, and we had to develop internal review systems to swing things the other way.

It really was tough for a while. But it was all part of the evolution and learning-journey about making all of this work for Zappos.

After all, no one had ever tried something like this in a company of this size. Ever.

And for those of us who saw how this was going to benefit the company in the long run, it was a very exciting time.

Arun Rajan
Chief Operating Officer
Before Zappos, the longest I worked anywhere was three years.

I worked at Travelocity when it was small and left when it became big.

I worked at other start-ups because I loved the dynamic, and left for the same reason.

I had been at Zappos for four years, the longest I'd stayed anywhere, working as Chief Technical Officer (CTO), when I decided to leave in 2013. It seemed to be getting too big for me. The company was entering that phase of silos, losing some of its ability to be nimble, losing the excitement of charting new paths in the world.

What Tony wanted was to continue Zappos with the mentality and energy and growth possibility of a start-up, and to do so even when the company was at scale. But we weren't there, and I wasn't sure I wanted to stick around to see if we could get there. There was talk of self-organization, but I just wasn't convinced that it would work. So I made the decision to leave. It wasn't easy! It was emotional. I had become friends with Tony and Fred, and those friendships continued after I left. I saw them on the weekends. And I kept talking to them about these issues.

Obviously, Zappos wasn't a start-up when I joined in 2009, but I joined the company because I was fascinated and attracted to the idea that a company at scale could still care for its customers, employees, and community—simultaneously—while delivering fantastic business results unencumbered by traditional silos. But by 2013, even with the move downtown, it really was starting to feel like a big company to me, with bureaucratic silos across marketing, tech, merchandising, and more. I felt like it was impeding us from succeeding and growing and delivering the way Zappos had in the past—and the forecasts we ran for the year ahead were bearing that out.

So I left Zappos. I moved to a much smaller company, and what became evident almost immediately is that even though it was one-*tenth* the size of Zappos, it was facing the same challenges. It made me think that if I'm going to work through these challenges anywhere, I'd rather be back at the place with the people and culture that I have always loved from the start.

I shared my frustrations with Tony and Fred, and in 2014 they finally said, "Why don't you just come back?"

That took me by surprise.

Emotionally, it felt right. I would be going back to this company that really cared about humanity in a way that I had never witnessed anywhere else in my career. Stepping out of Zappos for a bit reminded me how big a deal this is in corporate America.

Logically I also knew that Tony and Zappos were committed to brea-king down the silos and bureaucracy that had crept in and that they'd made this drastic change to self-organization as a way to change direction.

My only real hesitation with returning to Zappos was that I would be coming back and heading directly into one of the company's most challenging times. Growth was stalled, as was our profitability.

My emotional reasoning won out over every doubt.

I knew what lay ahead for this company would be incredibly challenging. But I also knew what this company was about—and I believed that what Zappos was about, at its core, was stronger than all of the typical forces that might be working against us.

With a start-up, I think people are all in it for a similar thing. There's a purpose. It's a group of people collectively rowing in the same direction. And it may not seem that way in day-to-day things, but overall, everyone at Zappos was here for some reason that brought them together, anchored on the values of the company. I think there's something unique about that, because what you see in a lot of other companies, at least what I've seen, are politics and agenda. There's no core fabric that unites people around something, like a bigger purpose or set of values—other than making money, or maybe selling to a bigger company.

Zappos had already made a lot of money *and* sold to a bigger company. Why would I believe that it could possibly return to the feel of a start-up again?

Here's the answer: because we were all still rowing in the same direction. Not that people were rowing in the same direction for profits as they would at a start-up. Obviously, we've got to make money, but we were in it together for *other* reasons, and I think mostly it's because everyone related to some subset of the Core Values.

Even so, would moving to self-organization and entering a new era of constant evolution be enough to bring us out of a hole and set us on a new course for a long-lasting future?

Management science hadn't been reinvented for eighty years.

What would happen if this didn't work?

What would happen if we didn't figure this out?

John Bunch

Organizational Systems and Advisor
to CEO Tony Hsieh

I'm 6'7" and I hit my head on a regular basis.

There really was a lot more to figure out than any of us anticipated.

If we look at this idea that we want to act more like a city, well, in a city there are no rulers—like, nobody's telling you exactly what to do—but there *are* rules. There is a framework and some mechanics to how things get done. There are permitting offices and zoning boards and so forth, but there is no one person telling you "This is the way that X, Y, and Z have to be," or "This is what you have to work on," or "This is what you have to do."

It's interesting to apply this to business. In a city, if somebody wants to do something way outside the box, they're going to have to get a variance or go through some sort of clearance. But if they're just opening a new shop, they can just kind of go through the necessary processes and paperwork and do it. No one's stopping them.

Our idea is to run our business that way, too.

You can put two dry cleaners on the same block in New York City, and both of those dry cleaners can be successful. Maybe one uses old-fashioned chemicals; one uses more Earth-friendly chemicals. They cater to different customers, they have adamant fans and detractors and people who are loyal to one or the other, and some people go to both—they don't really see the difference; they just want their shirts done quickly and don't want to have to walk too far. Those people will go to whichever shop doesn't have a line that day. But if both businesses are thriving, and both are providing services to clients who need those services, tell me: Who loses? Nobody. And the vibrancy of those two businesses thriving right next to each other is good for the city.

The city's responsibility is to make sure those businesses have all the electricity and water supply and whatever other infrastructure they need to get the job done. Here at Zappos, I lead a team called "Infrastructure," and we're trying to make sure that everybody here can do what they need to do. Because, last I checked, we're the largest company to ever adopt Holacracy, and we learned pretty quickly that there are a lot of gaps in the system. We laid the groundwork and built the operating system almost overnight. Another analogy is that we laid the roads. But there are so many other connective tissues, such as the electricity and the sewer system, that have taken years to connect and build to make everything run smoothly.

And that's challenging, because we're trying to transform the organization while we operate the organization at the same time. We can't shut the city down just to put in the new sewer system, even though we really need that system. But if we want to be around in a hundred years, or a *thousand* years, we know we have to do this. We *have* to set up a resilient organization that operates more like a city.

The press gave our move to self-organization a lot of attention that first year. It was a pretty radical thing for a company of our size to do. But it was just a start for us. Right after we announced it, we were already looking ahead to how to fulfill a bigger goal, and that was to go Teal.

Holacracy is a tool, a framework. An operating system.

Teal is the container that Holacracy rests in—the broader purpose and vision of where we're trying to go.

Teal is the goal of that constant evolution.

The term "Teal" comes from a book called *Reinventing Organizations* by Frederic Laloux. The subtitle of that book is a little heady: "A Guide to Creating Organizations Inspired by the Next Stage in Human Consciousness," but it really drives at where we're headed. Where we've *always* been headed.

Laloux basically assigned colors to different types of organizations that currently exist. More static organizations are "orange" or "green" or "blue." But he posits that a new type of organization is emerging, and he calls that style of organization "Teal," which coincides with a new-age term for the next stage of human enlightenment.

Teal is about being self-organized. It's about wholeness. It's about evolutionary purpose.

I use a diagram when I give talks about this subject, and I describe the five basic organizational shifts that Teal organizations are making:

1. How to think about not just being for profit, but for purpose
2. Trying to think about moving from hierarchies to networks
3. How to move from controlling to empowering
4. How to move from planning to experimentation
5. And how to move from privacy to transparency

Holacracy helps us do some of those things, but not all of those things, because Holacracy still has hierarchy built into it.

In the core, out-of-the-box form of Holacracy, each circle has a parent circle, and that parent circle has a parent circle, all the way up to the General Company Circle (GCC). So it's still a form of hierarchy. It's not a hierarchy of individuals but of circles. And each circle has a lead link, who does have decision-making authority, though it's designed to be distributed and limited. As much as we try to move away from top-down control with Holacracy, it still sprouts up.

Where we want to get to, and what Tony was anxious to move us toward as quickly as possible, is a flattening of that structure— where each circle acts as its own micro-business.

We wanted to find a way to figure out how we could still have a Zappos government of sorts, making policies and doing what any city government would do. And no matter what, the Core Values wouldn't go away. Every employee would still have to align around those values. But what did we need to do to give our employees as much autonomy as possible? To get the hierarchy out of the way and to allow each circle to truly act as an independent microenterprise that would move as nimbly as a start-up does when it's new, and fresh, and manageably small?

We didn't have all the answers. Nobody had all the answers! This really was new territory. And forging into new, uncharted areas isn't for everybody. Not every employee wants to be an adventurer who's ready, willing, or able to hack through the jungle with a machete. And that is sort of what it felt like here at Zappos, especially during the first year of the changeover.

Maritza Lewis
Engage Team
I've fire-walked twice. Yes, it hurt . . . both times. ☺

There was a lot of resistance to self-organization. Like, a lot more than some of us expected. We seemed like a pretty nimble company. We'd made the move downtown. Those of us who'd been here a while, and there were a lot of us, had weathered some storms and had always come through just fine. But there was something different about this. The drastic change that sort of flew in the face of what most people know about running a business just caught some people really off guard. And the resistance didn't dissipate much over the course of the first year. People misunderstood how governance was supposed to work, and so they got all bogged down waiting for answers for things from the GCC when they should have just done what they wanted to do. It was supposed to be a case of "ask for forgiveness, not permission." But a lot of stuff just seemed to get bogged down.

Finally, at one of our All-Hands Meetings, Tony stood up onstage and said that he understood that our new way of organizing the company was creating confusion, and that we needed to take a step in a slightly different direction. That was when the concept of Teal came about. He really pushed it—I got the sense that he thought everyone would breathe a sigh of relief.

That was not what happened. Not at all. Some people got even *more* panicky. When it really set in that there were no more "managers," a lot of people who were managers got angry. People were losing their titles and their authority over others. It didn't seem to matter that they were gaining autonomy and the ability to put together new teams and oversee those teams as they pleased, which should all be really good things. It just felt to some people like they'd had the rug pulled out from under them. There was a lot of frustration.

And the thing about Teal is there is no way it's going to work unless everybody's on board.

So Tony sent out a company-wide email and made everyone an offer. An offer that would become known in Zappos history as the "Teal Offer."

It was based on the same famous "offer" that all Zappos new hires receive after going through NHT: a significant monetary proposal to leave Zappos if they feel that Zappos isn't a fit for them. Only in Tony's Teal Offer, anyone who decided they didn't want to continue the journey of self-organization and going Teal could feel free to leave with enough security that they would be able to start over in pretty much any way they chose: a severance of at least three month's salary, or one month's salary for every year they'd been with the company, whichever was higher.

It was a move that said, "We're doing this, and we need everyone on board." But it was also a move born of empathy, in service to our own employees, which showed the generosity and sensitivity of our leadership in realizing that this was a *huge* change and that it might be too much for some employees to make.

It. Was. Wild.

I swear you could hear a collective gasp echo all over Downtown LV.

I was here in November 2008, before the Amazon acquisition, when we went through a really rough time and had to lay a bunch of people off. That was an awful day. It happened to fall on my birthday, which made it twice as bad. There were several very sad "happy hours" going on around town. I will never forget this my entire life: Alfred Lin, our CFO at the time, walked the floor, up and down, every single aisle in CLT, just checking on people, and people were crying on his shoulder.

I don't want to lessen that layoff in any way because it really was devastating—but the Teal Offer was much, much worse.

Employees were given some time to make their decision. So it just turned into the longest goodbye, just an ongoing drip, drip, drip of loss and tears. Out of the blue, just when I thought I'd heard it all, one of my closest friends and colleagues would pull me into a room and say, "Okay, I'm gonna take the offer." And I would be like, "Oh my God. But you've been here for ten years!" And their response would be, "Yeah, but with what they're about to pay me, I can move my family back to the East Coast." Another coworker moved to Mexico to start her own little comedy club. One of our trainers who had been with the company for twelve years at that time had just earned her real estate license, and she said, "No, this is a sign. I need to do this" and "No hard feelings for Zappos."

It was enough money for people to go chase a dream, which is just so very Zappos in its own way. It was a tremendous service to those people who didn't want to stay. A tremendous opportunity for them. But a lot more people took the offer than I think even Tony might have anticipated. We lost 18 percent of our workforce, just like that.

Eighteen percent!

The Teal Offer was meant to move us forward by allowing people who didn't embrace self-organization to leave gracefully, but we wound up losing some of our senior managers and other people who had been with the company for a very long time. They simply felt it was an offer they couldn't refuse.

Watching all of those longtime employees walk out the door was devastating. It felt like we were losing family members, and they were leaving us *by choice*.

Honestly, I think a lot of us who stayed had some very real doubts about our future. About the *company's* future.

How would Zappos survive this?

The whole thing felt like a great big mess.

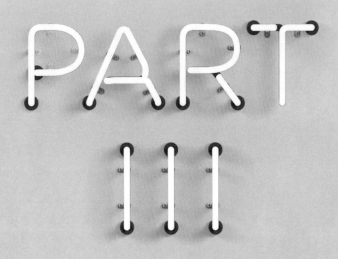

PART III

Creating

EARLY ADAPTERS

Christa Foley
Head of Brand Vision, Head of Talent Acquisition, and Head of External Culture Training

Born and raised in Vermont. Possibly one of only three people in Las Vegas who can say the same. And I know the other two from high school.

Christa self-proclaims she's not very good at math. I know for sure there are more than three people that say they were born and raised in Vermont. That may not actually be true, but they say it. Who knows why, that's a weird thing to lie about.

Nurturing is hard.

Having the patience and foresight to prune plants back, even when they appear to be healthy, believing that they'll come back even stronger—there's an element of faith in that effort.

Knowing when to replant. Planting bulbs in the fall that won't bloom until spring. Planting trees that you know might not grow for years. It's hard!

Cultivating a truly great garden takes time and effort, focus and attention, trial and error, and more. Will new technology make it better? Or are tried-and-true methods the way to go? What about hydroponics? Who needs soil, right? But how does that alter the flavor of the fruit?

Okay, maybe I'm taking Tony's greenhouse analogy a little too far. The point is, when a garden is properly cultivated, everything grows. And what was about to pop out of the soil here at Zappos was the start of a whole new era of creative thinking and creative endeavors.

Those who stayed, those who came aboard to fill positions after the Teal Offer, and those who took the Teal Offer and later came back (we've seen a surprising number of those!) would find opportunities here to do new things. To *try* new things. To unleash their own original ideas and grow them under a support system like nothing any of us had ever seen—because before that moment, a system like the one we were actively creating had never really existed.

So first, how I got here: I read Delivering Happiness, and after I finished reading the book I said to my boss at the time, "I'm leaving the company."

I worked for a family-run pharmacy in Long Island, and my boss looked at me puzzled and said, "Where are you going?"

"Well," I said, "I just read this amazing book and this company called Zappos is located in Vegas, where my high school friends live. It seems like everyone at this company is having a great time, and I'm going to go get a job there."

"Are you f—ing kidding me?" he said. "You're, like, the best employee I have! This is nuts."

He really thought I was crazy. He tried to offer me more money, but I said no. I applied at Zappos, and a month or so later they hired me. I drove cross-country with "Zappos or Bust!" written on the back of my car window and I had people honking at me and smiling and giving me the thumbs up pretty much the whole drive out here.

That was 2012. I got here right before the move downtown, right before the transition to self-organization, and I spent those first few years in Customer Loyalty before moving to Stevie's team, which does employee engagement, events, and charitable outreach. I started out buying promotional items and running the rewards recognition and programs team. So I was in charge of buying the pens, lanyards, beer koozies, t-shirts, mugs, and all sorts of swag that we gave away at events or that our employees bought internally to gift to clients or vendors. And one day I thought, "If I'm buying these promotional products, I bet we could save the company a lot of money if I actually started sourcing these promotional products direct from the manufacturer and cut out the middleman."

Because of where we were as a company, and what we were doing with self-organization, I didn't really ask anybody if I could do it. I just did it.

It started with race medals, like custom-made medals for road races or events we held for kids here on campus. We were paying something like $20 per medal at the time, and I thought, *That's nuts.* So I found a medal guy who would give us a better deal. And then I noticed we were paying a lot for t-shirts, so I found a local guy who could make t-shirts for me at less than half the price we'd been paying. Now I had a t-shirt guy and a medal guy. So when somebody asked me to order t-shirts or medals, I was like, "I gotta guy!" (I'm from Brooklyn, so "I gotta guy!")

Then I called up some manufacturers of some of the other products we usually purchased and I said, "Yeah, hi, I run a promotional products company called Swag Source," a name I completely made up, "and I'm interested in buying some of your product." They were happy to give me the wholesale pricing, and the prices were a lot lower than what we'd been paying the big distribution firms we'd been using for years. So I just kept going. I started sourcing all of these promotional products for the Zappos employees and selling them back to them at a much cheaper rate than they could ever get outside the company.

We use a lot of swag here. In the first three months that I tried this, from October to December 2016, I saved the company $100,000.

A hundred grand in savings. Real dollars. Actual cash.

WOW, right?

Not only did I save the company all that money, but then I started thinking: Why can't I just be the middleman and sell some of this stuff to other companies, too? The promotional products industry is a more than $23 billion industry. There's certainly room in the market-place for little ol' me. So that's what I started doing. I sold product at a huge savings to some of the charities and schools we work with, and other organizations. Not only was I saving the company money but starting to bring in some profit from this venture. Not much, but a little. We were saving money for nonprofit organizations at the same time, so that made them feel really good about the whole deal, too.

As time went on and people started to hear about "Swag Source," I started to sell this stuff on a bigger scale. And it's a great business because I don't even have to purchase and warehouse these products. I can truly act as a middleman, and the manufacturers will ship directly to my customers, which means there's very little overhead. And there was basically no start-up cost to do this, like, at all!

That's one way to view what happened with the whole move to self-organization and the Teal Offer: It took us one or two steps back to launch us five steps forward.

I turned this money-saving idea into a small business inside the company. And soon I needed to budget for someone to help keep track of the finances of it all, and someone else to help out because I was spending so much time on it, until finally my boss said, "Hey, we need to hire someone else for your position. This is taking up all of your time. Running Swag Source will be your new full-time job now, okay?"

So I created my own job!

The way I see it, I left a job I liked in Brooklyn, took a risk, and took one step back to start at an entry-level position at Zappos. But then after that one step back, I was able to take *five* steps forward.

And I think that's one way to view what happened with the whole move to self-organization and the Teal Offer here, too: It took us one or two steps back to launch us five steps forward. At least, that's what it felt like to me.

Miguel Hernandez
Art Curator and Creative
I'm a huge San Francisco Giants fan!

I've always had this thing about art and drawing and coloring, ever since I was a kid. I got into the Art Institute of California – Los Angeles when I was nineteen, and I pursued that for a semester or so, but learning about art in a structured way just wasn't for me. I just liked to draw and paint on my own. So I dropped out.

I'd always worked in service businesses—pizza shops, sandwich shops—and after my girlfriend and I moved to Las Vegas, I wound up being a bar manager for six years before I got sick of it. Like a lot of other people who discovered Zappos, I was burned out, sick of all of this structure that didn't make any sense, and sick of dealing with angry bosses and angry customers all the time. My girlfriend had actually started at Zappos first, and she loved it, and she encouraged me to apply. I made it, and I ended up working in the call center for three or four years. I loved it. I was so much less stressed, and we were making people happy all day long. It was great.

One thing we always do for customers is send them cards—we call them PEC cards, for the "personal emotional connections" we make with our customers—just as a thank you, to say, "Thank you for the conversation. Hope you like that jacket you bought," or whatever. And the cards they had available for us to send didn't really match my personality. So I started painting some handmade watercolor cards, landscapes and flowers and random things, and using those cards instead.

At one point the company ran a contest for new card designs, and everyone kept asking me to submit, and I did—and I won! They printed up some of my designs, and people started sending my cards out to customers. And people from other parts of the company started to notice, and they asked me to help design a flyer, or paint some signage for them, and I was always like, "Yeah, no problem!" I just loved doing it. It took up a lot of my time, but I didn't mind. Even on my lunch break, I would sit and do chalk art just for fun, and people really liked it.

Eventually, after we moved to the Downtown Las Vegas offices, they started asking me to do murals, like covering all the concrete walls on the basement level in an *Alice in Wonderland* theme. Or doing a wall in a conference room in a John Lennon theme, with a sketch of his face and a quote about dreaming. I wasn't getting paid extra for this. I just did it because I loved it, and having grown up in Los Angeles, I knew the effect of art on the environment and the culture, too. I love street art. I've seen how murals brighten up a whole neighborhood. I love, love, love color and can't stand boring, drab office colors. Color lifts people's moods, makes them do better in school—there are studies about this stuff. It really makes a difference. And I just knew it from where I'd grown up.

But it got to a point where I was doing so much artwork for other departments that it started to hurt my performance in CLT. They were actually going to discipline me at one point. Fortunately, this was right around the time we were making the switch to self-organization, so I went to the implementation team and told the lead link there, Jordan, what was going on. And he suggested I put together a proposal to change my job entirely, to create a new position where I could work on the art everybody wanted me to work on, full time.

"Really?" I said.

"You'll need to put together a proposal," he said, and he started explaining all this stuff that was like a giant puzzle. I'd never done anything like that. And he told me the proposal would have to go through governance, and they'd look at funding and ROI. I wasn't sure what the "return on investment" would be other than making the place nicer, continuing to create cards for customers, and that sort of thing. But I was all in. I was 100 percent invested. "Let's do this!"

I stopped doing art and just focused on this proposal when I wasn't fully engaged in the call center. It took me eight months to put it together. I was really nervous about it. I was so used to just taking orders. I'd never written anything to try to create my own career, especially one doing what I love. I felt like I had so much riding on that proposal.

I guess I wasn't the only one nervous, because we had an All-Hands Meeting and there were all kinds of tensions about self-organization and how it was working, or not working. And Tony was up onstage, saying, "Everything's okay! Everything's good. If you've gone through governance and turned every stone and you've hit a roadblock, email or text me. We're all in this together, and the idea is to free up the roadblocks, not create them. So don't be afraid to reach out."

I talked to Jordan, and he said he thought I was more than ready to submit this proposal, but because the work I was looking to do was outside of any one department, or any one circle, he thought I should send it directly to Tony. So I did. And I heard back from Jamie. She asked me some questions and said she would read the proposal and get back to me.

I was on the freeway a couple days later when I got a call from Jamie. "Congratulations!" she said. "You're our new Zappos artist!"

"What?!"

"Yeah. Tony saw your proposal, and he knows what you've done around here, and he said, 'Let's fund him. A hundred percent. Done.'"

I had to pull over. I was so happy. I asked to meet with Tony just so I could thank him and tell him I wouldn't let him or the company down.

I had some big dreams I put into that proposal. I said I wanted to spread art everywhere, not just for Zappos, but in the downtown community, and into the world. And this company embraced all of that. I've worked all over this building. In every conference room. In the nap room. I've done murals of iconic people, from Michael Jordan to Leonard Nimoy.

I don't want to get all spiritual and stuff, but a lot of these paintings—I put a lot of myself into them. And what I mean by "myself" is that energy, that transfer of energy. That energy that says I want to do something really good, but calm and warm. Work shouldn't be too serious. There are serious parts to it, but at the end of the day, these paintings say "you can still be yourself. You're a part of a bigger picture. You're not better than anybody else. We're all here chasing the same dream, trying to do the right thing, trying to be a part of this." I don't have the right words. I want people to interpret these paintings in their own way. But I pour a lot into them, and I do hope they have a positive effect.

Imagine if every company was open to finding what people are good at, what they love, and then funding them to do that thing.

I mean, I think they do. There's been so much support for the artwork I've done in the downtown area that the mayor actually named a day after me. It's hard to even think it's for real, you know? But Mayor Carolyn Goodman officially proclaimed May 16, 2016 as "Miguel Hernandez Day"!

Honestly, I never imagined I could have a job like this. Never. I thought I was just going to have to work for the rest of my life, just like my mom and dad always have.

Imagine if every company was open to finding what people are good at, what they love, and then funding them to do that thing. I can picture an entire workforce of muralists, artists, crafters, and painters. They could actually save companies so much money by creating things for the companies, from signage to toys and trinkets. You'd bring more jobs in and give these people benefits, because you trust them to create these things for you rather than outsourcing everything. You could even save paper costs, from flyers and advertising, by sending out artists to spread your message with chalk paint! I've got all kinds of big ideas. And the more Zappos keeps changing now, the more I keep thinking those ideas, those dreams of mine might actually turn into a business that's bigger than anything I ever imagined before I came here.

Chris Peake
Strategic Initiatives
I was an art major in college and my dream was to be an elementary school art teacher before Zappos came along.

Whether they consciously knew it or not, employees like Miguel and Regina were early adopters of the next phase of our move toward self-organization: the implementation of Market-Based Dynamics (MBD).

They saw a need for a service they could offer. They brought their ideas forth, managed to get their ideas funded, and then ran with them. They've both shown tremendous success in their own ways, and they stand as great examples of what can happen when people are allowed to bring their whole selves to the workplace; what can happen when a company listens to the ideas and recognizes the talents of its own employees; and what can unfold when you let your employees climb out of their boxes and give them the support they deserve.

Think about it: Regina probably could have gone outside the company, gotten a loan from her parents or even a bank with the research she'd done here at Zappos, and started her own Swag Source business on the outside. But she didn't have to. She had all the support she needed to launch that business right here, in a way that would benefit both her and the company—and even her outside customers, especially the charities and schools she was able to sell to at a discount.

Miguel, too. He's been hired to paint some pretty prominent murals in Downtown Las Vegas by people who saw his work here on campus. I have no doubt that he could have walked away from this company and probably made a great living on just his artwork after things started really happening for him. He would have been self-employed and might have wound up struggling to pay for health insurance and other costs that are such a burden to sole proprietors, but, even then, I think he could have made it. He's just so talented. But the point is: Under our new model, he didn't have to. He found the support he needed to do what he loves *right here*. Without giving up his job, his benefits, any of it. And we benefit from all of that, too! And honestly, that's just the beginning.

The ideas behind self-organization and what we're aiming toward with Market-Based Dynamics is a business in which this sort of independent growth of employees can happen all the time. We want to give any team in this company the freedom to start their own business. We want to give any individual in this company the freedom to chase their bold ideas, express their talents, launch a business, and maybe build a whole new team within Zappos to pursue ideas that none of us have even considered yet.

With any change, like any major shift in the way people think or with the implementation of any new tools or processes, you have some early adopters. People who just easily say, "Yes! We're all in. Let's do this. Let's figure it out. Let's help build the infra-structure. We care enough about Zappos that we're willing to create extra work for ourselves right now to build something for the future of Zappos, and the future for ourselves, because we believe in it that much." But then there are other people, and I think maybe the majority of people, who hear about a new initiative like Market-Based Dynamics and think, "No. Leave me the f—k alone. I'm gonna do my job and I don't want to hear about this MBD stuff. You talked to us about Teal, you talked to us about Holacracy. We moved downtown. What more do you want from us?!"

Those people need to hear the big success stories before they sign on and say, "Yes! MBD is for me! I've got a new business idea; here it is!"

That's fine. We don't want or need everyone to jump in right this very second. And not everyone on staff is an entrepreneur or an artist at heart. But I think once they see a couple of million-dollar or even billion-dollar ideas emerge from this in the next five years, people are going to get really excited.

At the end of the day, we don't need everyone in this company to be Tony Hsieh. We just want all of our employees to feel free to think of ideas. Of how they can better their customer service or even just to think about how and why we do things, like, "I've been making widgets for five years. Are these widgets valuable for my customer?" We want our employees to ask that, and if the answer is "no," we want them to go, "Cool. This thing is just not popular anymore and no one's buying it. Maybe I should make something else."

Entrepreneurialism is not necessarily thinking of the next billion-dollar idea. It's thinking about filling voids. It's thinking about service to customers, service to people. There are customers right here within the building. They're next door. They're every-where! So to whom can we provide better service? And I think if we approach it from that point of view, we're going to find holes that need filling, and we're going to find things that people need, which we can deliver. This is no different from what we've always done as a company, who we are, and where our core values and purpose have always driven us. It's just taking service to the next level.

People think, "Oh, I need to have all these really crazy ideas to be an entrepreneur," but really all it comes down to is taking your one idea and doing something about it. It's important to remember that you can have a million ideas, but if you keep them in your head and never share them, and never make a move, nothing is ever going to happen.

We want to provide the support for our employees to let those ideas out and to take a step toward turning them into reality.

Of course, that means taking some risks. But there are also risks if we don't do anything at all, right? Just staying the course and doing nothing but supporting our e-commerce business is eventually going to be a dead end. E-commerce will change. Maybe 3-D printing will become so fast and cheap that people will make their own custom footwear and clothing at home in a few years and all the shoe stores and clothing stores in America will go out of business. Maybe people a hundred years from now will stop wearing shoes because they want to be closer to nature. I don't know!

But not taking an action is still an action. No matter what, we aim to be proactive.

In a lot of ways, Zappos is like every other company. We have our problems. And problems can only be solved by taking action. But we also have a tendency of swinging the pendulum way too far to the left or to the right sometimes, and we want to figure out where the middle is, so that all of these bold ideas can succeed.

The "do whatever you're passionate about" messaging that we shared with employees about Teal was a perfect example. The idea that everyone could just do what they want without broader context or the proper constraints doesn't work. There's too much chaos. There are too many things pulling people in different directions. You can't just expect that humans are going to go out and do the right things for the business if given no rules or constraints, because they don't always do that.

So we have to put some guide rails on how this all unfolds. And through Market-Based Dynamics, we're going to accomplish that.

Going forward, we're asking everyone at Zappos to balance their own circle's profits and losses. And how does one account for P&L in a marketing department, or customer service, or circles that aren't actually selling anything? By creating a "market" economy within the business. Basically, each circle will start with a budget, and then whatever goods and services they need from other circles—be it printing, or design time, or collaborations of some kind—they'll have to "buy" and "pay for" those services.

If a circle can't seem to sell its existing services to any other circle in the company, then maybe that circle shouldn't be given budget for those services every year, and instead should figure out different services to provide that create more value for the company. It's not like we're going to fire the people in those circles that don't do so well. We'll just work with them to realign or combine with other circles that need more help. But for the most part, the inner workings of Zappos itself are being positioned to act more like a free-market economy. More like businesses would act within a city.

Of course, we have to have parameters and constraints, and these constraints are what we've been building for the last few years. And the constraints come from trial and error and the lessons we've learned from the past. It's nice to think that we could say, "Hey, we have ten core values and we have these profit goals that we need to hit that we committed to Amazon. So go do what you please!" In an ideal world people would do the right thing and align around that and actually move the business forward. But the truth is, there are outliers. When there were no constraints, we've wound up with people sleeping in the basement and people wanting to raise llamas on campus. So as we do this, we know we need to have the right communication— just as we did during the move to Downtown LV—and that communication has to be focused on making sure that people are aligned around what Zappos is trying to achieve.

And then comes the really cool part: Once these budgets are in place, once every circle is responsible for its own P&L, every one of those circles has the freedom under self-organization to go ahead and invest in people's ideas. Let's say Regina had the idea to expand her business to another product; say she wants to source and sell office products at a discount to nonprofits (I'm completely making this up) the same way she did with the swag items. And let's say Stevie's team didn't want to fund that idea. Regina would now be free to go and pitch that idea to any circle, *any* team within Zappos, to see if another team might like her idea enough to help fund it and get it going.

It has the potential to become like an in-house bazaar full of mini start-ups and venture capital firms.

Everyone within Zappos will now be free to be an entrepreneur, and every team within Zappos has the opportunity to partner in and profit from these entrepreneurial ideas. That means there will be competition. There will be risk. There will be trial and error. There will be all sorts of communication and budgeting and cross-talk between departments and circles—all but eliminating *any* possibility of silos. And there will be, hopefully, a feeling here of all sorts of energetic start-ups getting off the ground all at once, all the time, that will help Zappos grow into the future in unstoppable ways that we might not even be able to envision at this moment in time.

> *There will be competition. There will be risk. There will be trial and error. There will be all sorts of communication and budgeting and cross-talk between departments and circles—all but eliminating any possibility of silos.*

And all that will be done with 200 percent accountability, because each and every circle will be responsible for its own P&L, and all of the circles (or teams) combined will be responsible for making sure that Zappos as a whole continues to meet its profit and growth targets for Amazon.

That said, Zappos' Core Values, and our culture, and the way we've always been focused on service, all of that remains fully intact. If we don't deliver the best service and experience of what we're doing, then there's a problem, right? So we can't just start a run-of-the-mill swag business. We need it to be *great* and to deliver service that's worthy of the Zappos name. If we think bigger and we start a Zappos cable company (again, I'm just making this up!), we need to make sure we blow all of the competing cable companies out of the water in terms of customer service.

No matter how big or small the idea might be for a new business, from doing in-house food delivery for a few bucks' profit, to launching Zappos Airlines or Zappos Hotels—whatever the future may bring—the Core Values and especially our dedication to value number one, "Delivering WOW through Service," must remain at the foundation of everything. Because we all know that's what will make these new businesses succeed.

THE EVOLUTION
REVOLUTION

Rachel Murch
Strategic Initiatives
I can sing all the states in alphabetical order. It's
a great skill that comes out while drinking. ☺

To me, moving to self-organization felt like a natural evolution. I know it took a lot of people by surprise, but I didn't think of it as a new idea. I thought of it as the next step in an idea that was planted a long time ago.

The way that I describe it is that Tony is always ten years ahead of everyone else, and so he kind of had this vision a long time ago, way before us. And so everything that we've introduced at Zappos is a part of getting us to his vision.

In early 2011, I started working with Tony when he asked for help starting a program called Z-Frogs, which was inspired by his time as cofounder of a venture-capital (VC) firm called Venture Frogs before his time at Zappos.

> In 1996, I cofounded an online advertising company called LinkExchange with my college roommate Sanjay. We grew the company to about 100 people and ended up selling the company to Microsoft two and a half years later for $265 million. I used some of the funds from the sale to cofound and invest in Venture Frogs (we called it an angel fund) in 1999. We invested in twenty-seven different internet companies, of which Zappos just happened to be one of them, and my initial role was just as an adviser and investor to Zappos. Over the course of the next year, I realized that for me, investing was pretty boring, and I missed being a part of building something on a day-to-day basis. Out of all the investments we had made at Venture Frogs, Zappos was both the most promising and the most fun, so I ended up joining Zappos full time in 2000.

TONY

The idea was to bring the best practices he learned from that model into our company, with the belief that good ideas can come from anywhere. He created an internal VC in which he and three other executives sat on a panel and employees were able to pitch ideas to them—to help move the company forward or to present new and innovative things. It was his way of creating this culture of innovation and giving people the opportunity to really contribute to the future of Zappos, whatever it looked like.

Granted, at that time he didn't outline this vision of "Zappos could be an airline" or "Zappos could sell swag" or "Zappos could be a whatever," but that was what he was really getting at.

It was one of many seeds he planted to give people an opportunity to pitch ideas and then potentially get funding, or even get a whole new job. So I would say what we've been doing these last few years is just a part of the last twenty-plus years of the Zappos evolution. We like to say that Zappos is a customer service company that just happens to sell [blank].

Holacracy was a part of the evolution, as was the Teal Offer—trying to keep people at the company who were really committed to this vision. And then we moved to what our main project is these days, which is this world of Market-Based Dynamics. Introduced in 2017, MBD is our current initiative to help teams act like a micro-business within the Zappos business. It's our next step in the evolution to become a more self-organized company.

One foundational layer of self-organization, and operating like a micro-business, is the opportunity and responsibility of managing the financial aspects of that business. It was necessary to reinvent how budgets were handled in a self-organized and market-based environment. In late 2018, we introduced Customer-Generated Budgeting (CGB). This helped Zappos create a networked economy, allowing teams to quickly adapt to the needs of their customers, both internal and external. Feedback loops increased (compared to top-down budgeting), helping Zappos to be more resilient in an unpredictable market environment. CGB also allows for new ideas and innovations to be funded internally from customers or teams anywhere within the organization.

So much of my time is spent communicating with our employees, trying to help people rethink their mindset about the value that they're adding to the company. And part of it is new ideas—innovation and creativity and all of that—but that's not all of it. It's also about being financially responsible. How do we make sure that we're making good decisions for the company, so that we can do these other really cool things? Whatever those things are, we don't know. To help with this communication, we recently introduced the concept of the Triangle of Accountability. Part of the purpose for creating the Triangle of Accountability was to come up with the minimum number of constraints to enable maximum freedom and accountability. As long as each circle is within the three boundaries—is in line with our culture and core values, provides the very best customer service and experience, and balances their profits and loss—any circle or team can do whatever they want.

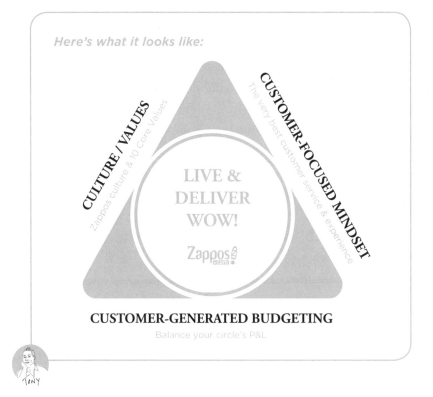

Here's what it looks like:

CULTURE/VALUES
Zappos Culture & 10 Core Values

CUSTOMER-FOCUSED MINDSET
The very best customer service & experience

LIVE &
DELIVER
WOW!

Zappos

CUSTOMER-GENERATED BUDGETING
Balance your circle's P&L

It's not a simple task. Even though we hire people who we believe will be able to adjust and realign with wherever we go, it still takes work. Especially since we're really inventing this new model as we go. No one has done this before. No one! And that's super exciting, as long as you see it as part of the Zappos evolution—that all of these pieces are aligned and in fact that all of them go back to putting service first. Because all of this is about providing great service to customers, clients, shareholders, and especially our own employees, who ultimately will have much more say over their own fates and futures because of where we're headed.

Everything that we're doing is an amplification and extension of our core values.

And I think some of the people that left with the Teal Offer saw what that was worth, pretty much as soon as they left this company. And that's why some of them came back.

> *We call those Zappos employees who left and came back "Zoomerangs."*

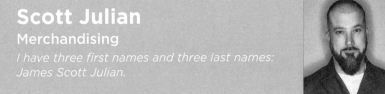

Scott Julian
Merchandising
I have three first names and three last names: James Scott Julian.

I took the Teal Offer. I convinced myself that I needed this change.

Another company came along around the same time and offered me a significant salary increase over what I was making here. Really significant. It seemed like too big of a coincidence. How could I refuse such an amazing thing? I had been here a lot of years, and I remember thinking, *I have to go out into the world and prove to myself that I can be good somewhere else.* So I took the Teal Offer—and I took the other offer—and I left.

The first sign that I'd made a mistake was when I got to Seattle and, big surprise, it was raining. I'd grown to love the dry weather in Las Vegas. Seattle was the opposite. Plus, I had friends in Vegas. I knew no one in Seattle. So right off the bat, it just wasn't good. The weather and my friendships were two parts of my core happiness that couldn't be replaced with double the salary. There's a big difference between making enough money and thinking you need more money. A big difference. Enough money is sometimes the thing that's way more important.

Then, in this new company, the culture was immediately different. Everything was more corporate. There was a 9 A.M. meeting every morning. Every morning. Why? Every morning, everyone gathered in a room for like three minutes and . . . what? Nothing. If you had questions, they had to be asked at a later time, in another setting—probably another meeting. It just made no sense to me. It was a waste of time that meant nothing and accomplished nothing, for anyone. And that's how they started every day.

In just the first two or three months I was there they hired three to four more executives. I think one thing that Zappos always did really well was to hire the executive levels really slowly. We always believed in building the culture, which meant really taking the time to make sure we were bringing in the right people. This other company didn't even hire people with the right background. Like, at Zappos, if we're hiring you to buy shoes, you probably have some experience buying shoes. But this other place, like a lot of places, would hire a new executive who'd previously sold shark fins, just because he was a "good businessman" in somebody's eyes.

I remember running into my former Zappos colleague, Eileen, at a market in New York about six months into my new job, and she asked me what it was like. I said, "Yeah . . . it's just not the same." I knew I was unhappy already.

At the new place, even six months in I felt like I had no one I really wanted to spend time with outside the office. I thought about the amount of money Zappos invested in happy hours in any given week, and it was about the same amount of money this new company planned to spend on the one annual outing for their employees in any given year. There was just no chance anyone was going to bond in that place, ever.

Plus, the CEO drove a really expensive exotic car. Like a supercar. The whole idea of it just rubbed me wrong. We have people who live by example at Zappos. Tony himself drove an old Mazda, or an Acura or something, and wore a t-shirt to work. (At the time this book is being written, Tony doesn't even own a car. He gave it up—to an employee who won it during a raffle to celebrate the company move downtown. He moved to an Airstream Park just a mile or so down the street so he could walk to work.) It was just all so different. In the end, I decided to leave that company and go get a different job, and it very quickly turned into more of the same.

Then, a year and a half after I'd left, I got into a really serious motorcycle accident. Someone was texting on their phone—don't ever text and drive. I was really a mess. It was three weeks later before I could perform normal tasks. When I finally went home to heal, a day or so later a UPS truck pulled up in front of my place, and the guy rang my bell, and in his arms he held a great big box from Zappos. I hadn't ordered anything since I left—out of guilt, I think. So I had no idea what was in this box.

When I opened it, I couldn't believe my eyes. Honestly. I tear up just thinking about it. It had been more than a year and a half that I'd been away at that point, but the whole floor got together and filled this box with things they knew I loved—my favorite liquor, just all sorts of stuff that was meant just for me, to wish me a speedy recovery and let me know they were thinking of me.

To be fair, I did get a basket from my new company as well. A basket from Hickory Farms. I like Hickory Farms—I mean, who doesn't? But it wasn't personal, you know? How could it be? There was nothing personal about that company. But for the people I used to work with at Zappos to get together and do something so caring, and so personal, even after I'd been gone for so long—that was huge to me. It was a turning point. It just got me thinking, "What am I doing here when my friends and my family and my happiness are back in Vegas?"

So I came back. Thankfully, they took me back. They took me back with open arms, and I'll never leave this place again. I really won't. This place treats people the way people ought to be treated. All people. Plain and simple. And that matters more than double the salary anywhere else, that's for sure.

Joe Grusman
E-Commerce Marketing
I am a mechanic and a lawyer.

The fact that we welcomed Scott and a whole bunch of other former Zappos employees back into the fold after they'd taken the Teal Offer says a lot about our company culture. For each of these individuals, taking the offer was a risk. It was a big change. It was an experiment. And in some cases, they found that the experiment failed. They learned from it. They came to understand that what they had was somehow better, more appealing, more in service to their needs and their lives than what they thought they would get somewhere else. That's a great lesson! A valuable lesson. They're better for having gone through that experiment and finding a conclusion. That's way better than if they'd never taken the risk to venture out in the first place.

Experimentation through trial and error is a big thing here at Zappos, a big thing in any Teal organization, and a super important part of building a resilient workplace.

We *want* people to make mistakes. We *want* people to *fail*!

In the Holacracy framework, we have all of these different circles, and most of the circles are made up of just three or four people, with parent circles that cover larger groups, and so on. And because of this framework, each of the smaller circles is able to move and make decisions and adjust the way a small start-up might move. And that's a great thing.

As the lead in marketing, I tell our team, "I'm the safety net. You need to go ahead and take this chance. If you fail, it's fine. But we need to fail forward fast."

We don't want anyone lingering in failure. We don't want to spend so much time on ideas that don't work that we lose track of other important aspects of the business. But we want to encourage people to experiment, which means encouraging them to go ahead and fail without fear of severe consequence.

> *Experimentation through trial and error is a big thing here at Zappos, a big thing in any Teal organization, and a super important part of building a resilient workplace.*

Our overall mentality here is absolutely "Go ahead and fail."

It's a start-up mentality. An experiment mentality. We know we can fail 80 percent of the time without worry, because the 20 percent that works is going to outweigh the other 80 percent that doesn't.

That's our approach, and it works.

For example, a while ago we had someone working on a search algorithm, manually, to see if we could beat the existing models with human minds and sort of prove that the algorithm wasn't working. This was for one of our paid-search campaigns, which we manage across Google and also Bing. Everybody forgets about Bing, but at the time this happened, Bing accounted for around 20 percent of searches, which is a lot.

Anyway, while they were working on this algorithm, they accidentally paused the paid-search results. The next day we came in and we were like, "What happened to the numbers? Why is everything askew?" And we looked into it and saw that it was paused.

We figure it cost us about $75,000 in sales, just overnight.

At another company, somebody might have been fired for that. But the idea here is, "Why would we ever fire you? One: You're never going to make that mistake again. And two: You just learned a $75,000 lesson."

> Our overall mentality here is "Go ahead and fail." . . . We know we can fail 80 percent of the time without worry, because the 20 percent that works is going to outweigh the other 80 percent that doesn't.

Why would I want to teach someone a $75,000 lesson, at my company's expense, and then let them take that lesson and put it to use at another company? It doesn't make sense. Plus, it showed us that we needed to put new systems in place to ensure that something like that wouldn't happen again. And guess what? It's never happened again. So that "mistake" was valuable to all of us.

In fact, the employee who made that mistake has since moved up and become a very strong leader within the company, adding even more value than we anticipated in all sorts of ways.

To fail forward fast and never rest on our laurels, to see mistakes as opportunities for growth and learning—that's the impetus behind so much of what we do here.

Jamie Naughton
Chief of Staff
I was hired two weeks before Christa Foley and I've spent the past decade coming up with fun ways to remind her of this fact. My latest: I found out I'm employee #70. She's #75.

*Mistakes happen. But mistakes in the context of self-*organization? Mistakes in the context of Market-Based Dynamics? Mistakes in a workplace that is now totally focused on learning, and growth, and humanity, and breaking new ground? Mistakes are opportunities.

There's an infamous Zappos story that comes to mind: One time there was some code that was written incorrectly and it put one of our biggest-selling brands on sale during the time when it sells the most products, right before the holidays. And we aren't talking about a minor discount; we're talking about this entire brand, every item, was put on *drastic* sale. Within an hour everyone started to notice. A wave of "What is going on?" washed over the whole building. The tech team figured it out and corrected it, of course—probably not much more than an hour later—but our holiday customers were quick to snap up that deal.

It wound up costing our company close to a million dollars. In one hour.

Of course, we have legal clauses to protect us when those types of things occur. Like most e-commerce sites and even supermarkets that print sale prices in their flyers, we have terms of service that say we're not responsible for errors or "misprints," and that we have the right to charge the actual price in the case of such an error. (Customers also have a right to cancel their orders if that clause kicks in.) That's great on paper, but we're a service company. Do we really want to pass this mistake on to the customer and send each of them an email saying, "Sorry! That price you paid was a coding error. We're charging you full price after all."

No! No way.

Those customers got the deal of the century. It was like winning the lottery for them, and I'm sure they told all their friends. As for us—well, no one lost their job over this incident, but we definitely learned a lesson.

Sometimes you make mistakes trying to push boundaries. And sometimes mistakes just happen. This was a big one, and, even though it was expensive, it was an opportunity for the company to learn from that error, document it, and find ways to make sure that same mistake wouldn't happen again.

Not all of our mistakes are in tech and coding. We made a ton of mistakes in our early days just trying to get sales. There's a story about us spending something like $30,000 to take out an ad at the home plate of a major sports stadium, and when we did the metrics we realized we got one customer from that ad. *One!* When that person came shopping at the site, we were all like, "Hey! That's our $30,000 customer!"

We all make mistakes, and that's okay. That's how humans learn. That's how we make progress. And now, as we embrace self-organization, we embrace our mistakes more than ever.

I don't think anyone would disagree that we made a lot of mistakes with the rollout of our self-organized system, but we still rolled it out. The fear of mistakes doesn't stop us. I think that is one of the best things about Zappos, and one of the hardest things—because we're constantly adjusting to new things. We're not afraid of change, so we just push it all the time. And with self-organization, we knew there was a ton that we hadn't figured out. We tried to put in some safeguards. We want to be smart about our mistakes, making sure our mistakes don't bankrupt the company, right? But allowing ourselves to make mistakes means we're able to learn and change and accomplish things faster than most companies could ever imagine. And that is absolutely one of the biggest keys to resilience and longevity.

Even the Amazon acquisition was a strategic move on our part to continue to focus on the long term. When you're working with most investors, it's all about the short term, and we knew that Amazon was and is a long-term thinker. So, these days, when we meet with the higher-ups, it's not a hard sell for us to say, "We're gonna try this new thing, and you can check back in six years. It may or may not work. We probably won't know for five or six years." And Amazon would say, "That sounds interesting!"

We're not a small company, but compared to Amazon we're tiny! So we have a lot of flexibility to kind of push the boundaries, and, as long as the premise of putting service first always applies, what we're doing usually makes sense to the folks at Amazon. They actually want to learn from our mistakes, as well as our successes, because they're interested in extending the longevity of their company, too.

So much of what we spoke about in the first part of this book, the core idea of customer service and thinking of the "customer" beyond just the paying customer, the employees, the vendors, all of it applies to what we're doing internally. The idea that business can be a win-win for everybody, that everybody should be served well by what's happening here—all of that ties in to these forward-thinking management moves we're making.

I think part of the story for the last ten years, at least in my journey at Zappos, is that we have grown up. Of course we still hang out, we're all friends with each other, we go out, we have the happy hours or whatever—but Zappos was never about the happy hours. Zappos was never about the "tech perks" that people want to talk about: the nap rooms, the pool tables, the music room. They're all secondary to what we were trying to create here, which is an environment where

> *Zappos was never about the happy hours, the "tech perks." They're all secondary to what we were trying to create here, which is an environment where people can flourish, an environment where people want to come to work.*

people can flourish, an environment where people want to come to work, an environment where you're proud of the brand and of your own accomplishments and the fact that we're working hard to make people happy.

So while we still get a lot of attention for our nap room (which features massaging lounge chairs set up under the peaceful curving walls of an enormous exotic fish tank, built by the guys from the TV show *Tanked*), and we still get attention for our happy hours (some of which recently moved to our new on-campus bar), it's the culture that really matters. The culture is the feeling, the personalities in the room. And I think in the last ten years we've really been focused on the humanness of us. Not just the fun stuff we do, but making sure our benefits are intact, that we can plan families, buy houses, do all the things that we're all working for—and we can do it in a place that *has* pool tables and nap rooms. A *fabulous* nap room.

The whole-human side of the workplace plays a big role in whether people are going to stick around for fourteen years and be happy in the work they do; it plays a big role in if they're going to want to create new things and go through the changes and the ups and the downs of implementing new ideas and new managerial structures. The fact that our company is trying to understand what people need to feel happy at work and to want to be a part of this organization for the long term, which means through having kids and families and all the various phases of life both inside and outside of work—that's huge!

I think many companies have good intentions, and they aren't purposefully trying to shortchange their employees or drive them to seek work elsewhere, but they have policies that prevent their intentions from finding their way into the everyday feel of the company. I mean, I can tell within five minutes of talking to a call-center rep how many handcuffs are placed on them and what their ability is to actually help me. It's pretty obvious that those employees are getting yelled at when the phones are off but are expected to be friendly to their customers. It just lacks sincerity. And if those employees aren't being taken care of and treated like the full human beings they are, there's no way they're going to give their all to the company in the long run. No way! It's just not going to happen.

And by no means are we saying we have all the answers, or our way is the only way. I hope that's clear. We're just figuring this stuff out as we go, and the ups and downs of the change to self-organization are proof of that. But way back when, a million years ago, when Tony first tried to explain the Core Values, he said, "It may seem sometimes like we don't know what we're doing, and it's true. We don't. But take comfort in knowing no one else knows how to build an online shoe company, either."

I still feel that way when it comes to developing an autonomous workforce and a self-organized company: "We don't know what the hell we're doing, but no one else knows how to self-organize a huge company or create Customer-Generated Budgeting, either!"

Customer-Generated Budgeting. That's pretty new around here. It's basically a way to make MBD work by eliminating the bureaucracy of the traditional, hierarchal budgeting process. So instead of a top-down system, where each division (or team, or circle) gets their annual budget from up high and the control of that budget rests with someone above from year to year, each individual circle is now in charge of their own budget. We've created a whole new system to make those budgets transparent and accessible.

So much of the push into self-organization was just about one thing: preventing unnecessary bureaucracy. We got a lot of attention in the business world for making this shift, and now, when someone rolls their eyes and says something like, "Oh, you're that company that implemented Holacracy," I just think, *Yeah, well, that's so 2014!*

Holacracy is just part of our job now. It's a framework. A platform, as John Bunch mentioned earlier. It doesn't even seem new to us anymore. In your company you have staff meetings on Fridays, and at Zappos we have Holacracy meetings every once in a while. It's not even something we talk about; it's just something we do.

In the beginning, it was clunky and it was hard, and no one knew anything about it, and now we all kind of make self-organization work the way our teams need it to work.

The goal of it all isn't to complicate things. It's to *simplify* things. We're always trying to keep unnecessary bureaucracy out of the way.

And the good news is, if we make a change and that change *isn't* working, we're not afraid to change it back, or to change it again, or to take whatever step is needed to undo the mistake we made. There's no hubris. There's no sticking with a bad plan just to save face or just because someone said so.

Trial and error. Experimentation. Keep it moving forward.

If self-organization wasn't working for us, we wouldn't self-organize anymore. Sure, the transition to it was noisy and clunky, and it did cause a lot of pain, and there were parts of it that had to be stepped back and readjusted on the fly. But overall, it's worked great. There were just some parts that needed to be adapted to who we are as a company, so we adapted those parts to fit.

For example, a completely self-organized system didn't work in the call center because, well, human nature. People don't want to work on the weekends. People want to choose shifts that fit with their schedules. But the company needs to have people on the phones 24/7 no matter what. So we were forced to step back into something a little closer to a traditional managerial hierarchy in CLT, just that one department, to make sure all shifts were covered no matter what. We couldn't have the call center empty every Saturday night. We just couldn't. That didn't serve our customers or our business. But we allowed the CLT circles to figure it out on their own. That was key. They worked on finding a solution together instead of sitting back and taking orders from on high.

Frankly, there are some teams that don't really do much with self-organization, and then there are other teams that can't live without self-organization. Some departments need one staff meeting per year and some departments have staff meetings every day. But every team here figures out how to make it work *for them*.

That makes such a difference on a human level. There's a lot less opportunity for resentment and more opportunity for ownership and pride in decision making, even when the decisions are tough.

Fun fact: Here's how Wikipedia defines self-organization:

Self-organization, also called (in the social sciences) spontaneous order, is a process where some form of overall order arises from local interactions between parts of an initially disordered system. The process can be spontaneous when sufficient energy is available, not needing control by any external agent. It is often triggered by random fluctuations, amplified by positive feedback. The resulting organization is wholly decentralized, distributed over all the components of the system. As such, the organization is typically robust and able to survive or self-repair substantial perturbation. Chaos theory discusses self-organization in terms of islands of predictability in a sea of chaotic unpredictability.

Self-organization occurs in many physical, chemical, biological, robotic, and cognitive systems. Examples of self-organization include crystallization, thermal convection of fluids, chemical oscillation, animal swarming, neural circuits, and artificial neural networks.

Self-organization is realized in the physics of non-equilibrium processes, and in chemical reactions, where it is often described as self-assembly. The . . .

TONY

concept has proven useful in biology, from molecular to ecosystem level. Cited examples of self-organizing behaviour also appear in the literature of many other disciplines, both in the natural sciences and in the social sciences such as economics or anthropology. Self-organization has also been observed in mathematical systems such as cellular automata. Self-organization is an example of the related concept of emergence.

Self-organization relies on four basic ingredients: (1) strong dynamical non-linearity, often though not necessarily involving positive and negative feedback, (2) balance of exploitation and exploration, (3) multiple interactions, (4) availability of energy (to overcome natural tendency toward entropy, or disorder).*

Okay, maybe it's not a fun fact for you, but it's a fun fact for me. ☺

Think about this: How often do people leave a company because the relationship with their boss, their direct boss—their manager—isn't good? Somebody who may be a great fit for your company might get so fed up that they actually *leave* because they don't get along with one person out of the hundreds or even thousands of people in your organization. That's a major fault in the traditional hierarchal system, isn't it?

There was a confused period when all the headlines read, "Zappos gets rid of bosses!" And then our employees sort of digested that news, right? But there was never an intention to not have bosses. The intention was to limit any one boss's ability to tell us what to do. We wanted our employees to have more autonomy. But within each division, within each circle, we still need someone to budget and manage resources and all of that. So

---

* Wikipedia contributors, "Self-organization," *Wikipedia, The Free Encyclopedia*, https://en.wikipedia.org/w/index.php?title=Self-organization&oldid=895249589 (accessed May 20, 2019).

the pendulum swung from everyone thinking, "No bosses, this is great!" to "Wait, no, this is what a 'lead link' does. That lead role is important. It's a 'boss,' but not in the traditional way."

Everybody has a different relationship with their lead link. Some lead links are a little more hands-on, and some are really hands-off. And some employees work well with a lead link who is hands-off, and some don't. And under the new system employees have much more leeway to figure out where they fit in or don't, and to find a fix that will keep them here—where in the old system the only "out" might have been to exit the company.

I mean, look at what happened with Miguel, and Johnnie, and even me! We're opening all kinds of doors to those sorts of opportunities to move into new positions and create whole new positions now. We're doing it all the time—because we know that's going to keep us nimble. It's going to make Zappos feel like a whole bunch of start-ups all under one roof.

What's even more exciting is it's really good for business.

There is nothing but upside to allowing your own staff to develop and grow.

I had a team meeting recently and I said something about the call center, and I looked around the room, realizing that 100 percent of the people in that room had started on the phones—so they all knew exactly what I was talking about. There was no disconnect. Though they no longer worked in the call center, they've all been there and understood it implicitly. And they've all had the opportunity to explore and evolve their passions as employees and as individuals.

All of our executive assistants at Zappos, all of them, came from the call center. And any and all of them now have the ability to grow and change and bring their whole selves, their best selves, into whatever they want to become here as we move forward—and that ability only grows the more we get the bureaucracy out of the way.

I think that brings this whole discussion full circle to what all of this change and innovation and difficult stuff we're trying to do here is all about: It's about bringing your whole self to work. That's the goal of our culture.

> *Do unto others as you would have them do unto you.*

The goal is not to grade everyone on how well they express the Core Values. And we realize that our particular set of core values isn't for everyone.

During one of the very first speeches I gave for Zappos, this woman, a total cynic, stood up and said, "Yeah, that's great. I work in a hospital. I can't stick a funny hat on my nurse and send her in to talk to someone who's dying." And my response was, "Then don't. Don't put a silly hat on her head. Why would you do that? That's *our* job. We wear silly hats and parade around the office sometimes, and you *don't* wear silly hats because you're talking to people who are dying. Figure out what's right for your environment."

That doesn't mean you can't have a healthy work environment because you're in hospice care. In fact, I think it's even more important to have a healthy work environment in a job that's so much more stressful, emotionally, than ours. But even *that* job is about delivering service, isn't it? At its core? Making people as comfortable and as happy as you can. Doing the right thing. Thinking of their needs and then, hopefully, exceeding them.

All of this comes down to the Golden Rule: "Do unto others as you would have them do unto you."

That's it. The answer to everything was figured out thousands of years ago!

Delivering great service in everything we do is *that*: It's the Golden Rule.

Giving our employees the ability to bring their whole selves to work, to express their talents, to grow as humans—that's the Golden Rule in action.

THE FUTURE, NOW

Arun Rajan
Chief Operating Officer
I taught my oldest daughter how to drive. While she was incredibly confident, it took her four tries to pass her test. Was it the driver or the teacher?

In October 2017, three years after I'd returned to Zappos, I stood in front of our entire staff at our All-Hands Meeting and spoke to them about the remarkable journey we'd made.

Even while anchoring to Holacracy, and adjusting to the Teal Offer's impact, and evolving constantly on a road to self-organization that no company anywhere near our size had ever attempted, we had done something pretty remarkable: We had delivered three straight years of increasing profitability.

I reminded them that at the start of that very same period, I had returned to the company to find our financials at an all-time low.

Many companies at our scale require external intervention to be turned around in such circumstances. A successful turnaround from within isn't generally the outcome given the silos, entrenched positions, and politics that most companies develop at scale.

So why were we able to do this? Why were we able to do all of this, all at once?

My reflections and observations suggest it was something deep in our DNA, and deep in our culture, that allowed all of this to happen.

I did an informal survey of people all across the company, and the universal agreement with that sentiment was overwhelming.

During those three difficult years, the company, everyone, in every role, worked hard to "Embrace and Drive Change." Collectively we were unafraid to "Pursue Growth and Learning," because we knew that the old ways of doing business were potentially nothing but a dead end—and we didn't want any of this to end. And perhaps most of all, we delivered WOW, no matter the situation. We never stopped caring for our customers, employees, or community despite everything that was going on—even when some of our employees didn't agree with the direction in which we were headed. Even then, we cared enough to put together an offer for those employees to leave with no regrets, to pursue their own passions and interests. We didn't "have to" do that. We

> We never stopped caring for our customers, employees, or community despite everything that was going on—even when some of our employees didn't agree with the direction in which we were headed.

did it in service to them. We did it because that's who we are. And when some of them decided to come back in the years that followed, we cared enough to welcome them back with open arms.

Our core values mattered when the chips were down and our very survival was at stake. And our resilience was found in the very thing that drives us: our service.

It was an emotional speech to make. It came just a few weeks after a man opened fire on concertgoers attending the Route 91 Harvest festival, just behind the Mandalay Bay Resort and Casino on the Las Vegas Strip. A few short miles from our office. Many of us had friends or family who were at that concert when it happened. Some of us knew people who died. And even if we didn't, it struck home. It was a terrifying event that affected every one of us, right where we live and work.

So on that day, in what was for the most part a business presentation, I told my Zappos family: "Despite the continuous self-doubt and anxiety as we pushed through this period of constant change, which forced me so far out of my comfort zone, I stuck with it because of the incredible support, caring, and resilience that's built into the fabric of Zappos. Our relentless caring for our customers, our employees, and our community—even in dark times—is consistently in line with the type of company I want to be a part of. Because being a part of something like this is incredibly fulfilling."

There were a lot of tears shed at that meeting.

There was a tangible, visceral understanding that what we do here is about much more than work.

> *Our core values mattered when the chips were down and our very survival was at stake. And our resilience was found in the very thing that drives us: our service.*

It's about making our work matter.

It's about giving our work purpose.

As individuals, in groups, as a company, on our own time, in our own ways, and organizationally, we responded to the tragedy in ways of which every one of us can be proud, I think, for the rest of our lives.

And as we emerged from that dark moment, we did so knowing that our company was growing stronger and more resilient by the day, because we were evolving and preparing for our own longevity, no matter what unexpected events the future may bring. We emerged believing that we would be here for our community, for our customers, and for each other for a long time to come.

Tony Hsieh
CEO
Some of my favorite things are campfires, playing with fire, group messaging, and going on overnight bus trips with friends.

Again, this next section you're about to read is based on interviews with me and ghostwritten by Mark. The content is accurate and represents my point of view, even though these may not have been the exact words I said in the interviews.

*Self-organization is really the only form of organiza-*tion that's proven itself in nature, from an evolutionary point of view, as far as human organizations are concerned. And just like with cities, which are essentially self-organized systems, the benefits of moving to self-organization include more innovation, more productivity, increased resilience, and standing the test of time.

Now that it's been twenty years since this company first got off the ground, I think it's safe to say that we are well on our way to getting to true self-organization. But I also feel it's safe to say there is a reason why no other company has accomplished it or really even tried it at this scale, and that's because the way to get there is nonintuitive and *hard*!

We first launched Holacracy in 2014, after running a small test program in 2013, which means it took almost six years to finally get to a point of what we hope will finally lead to the next level of self-organization: the implementing of Market-Based Dynamics through a system of Customer-Generated Budgeting. But this year, we finally pulled the switch.

What is the minimal number of constraints we need to put in place to give each circle of employees the maximum amount of freedom and the maximum amount of accountability?

People both internally and externally have asked us why we felt it was so important to move toward MBD, and to CGB, which is kind of a subset of that. And the shortest message that seems to make sense to people is that to pull this off, we needed to figure out the answer to an incredibly complex self-organization question: What is the minimal number of constraints we need to put in place to give each circle of employees the maximum amount of freedom *and* the maximum amount of accountability?

The answer we arrived at in the fourth quarter of 2018 is "three."

One constraint is staying true to our foundation, our core values, and our culture. So each and every circle in the organization must make sure that whatever they're doing has to be in line with that, or help build that.

The second constraint is our brand, which is customer service and customer experience. So we have to make sure that as we do this, every circle is focused on service and experience that lines up with the established Zappos brand.

And then the third constraint is that since every circle is basically going to become its own mini start-up, each circle needs to balance its P&L.

We drew these three constraints as a triangle, and we called it the Triangle of Accountability. And the basic pitch to employees and to anyone who's interested in learning what we're doing is this: "Within that triangle, you can do whatever the heck you want. But you must live within those constraints."

I know there are people who think this is all just some kind of wild experiment. But it's not. It's a very controlled experiment, an experiment with an existing parallel in the real world (a.k.a. cities): If we can achieve this act of establishing a self-organized system that acts very much like a successful city, then productivity will go up, as will innovation, as will our resilient ability to stand the test of time.

That leaves one last big question, which is "Can it also create profitability?"

If the three accountabilities I mentioned are true, then logically, it *has* to. There's no way for those three things to be true and for the organization to *not* be profitable, unless, I don't know, maybe it's a company of zero people.

The only way things could go wrong is if the circles aren't operating within those three constraints. If there are circles that aren't balancing their P&L, or there are circles that are trying to maximize their revenue while being mean to everyone, then those circles will be dissolved. In a healthy city, some businesses go out of business, but new businesses inevitably pop up to take their place, just as new circles can form within this system of self-organization at any time.

Our core values have been in place since 2006, so they're a given now. That's an easy accountability for pretty much anyone who works here to live up to. Same goes for delivering service, which predates even our core values. The only "new" accountability is having each circle be responsible for their own financials in a very direct way. And we've worked to put systems in place that will, over time, make it easy for everyone here to keep track of all that.

This Triangle of Accountability took us a long time to figure out, and even though it's relatively "new," we feel each of the three sides will stand the test of time. First, there's plenty of data to show that all things being equal, companies with the strongest cultures financially outperform companies that don't have strong cultures, over the long term. Which means that if you're thinking in the context of what's best for a company's profits over a five-to-ten-year-plus horizon, then I don't think there's any evidence that *not* caring about culture is beneficial.

It's hard to measure ROI on "culture" investments in the short term. But there's plenty of research on its impact over the long term. The real resistance most companies have to spending time focusing on culture is that they're only worried about the next quarter or, at best, the next year. I think the average CEO tenure is three and a half years, or something like that. And if the average CEO is there for three and a half years, then they're only going to maximize for those three and a half years.

As for the longevity of the customer service side of the triangle, we have the history to back that up. Measurable, long-term ROI for every customer who enjoys the Zappos experience is strong, and especially for those whom we've helped when something went wrong. As Arun mentioned earlier, there's a 2× to 5× long-term increase in value with that subset of customers.

So there's only one side of the Triangle that is "untried." And when it comes to Customer-Generated Budgeting, which is the framework through which Market-Based Dynamics will freely work in this organization, there's plenty of proof out in the real world that markets work. And *markets* are what create innovations. I recommend reading a book called *The Origin of Wealth* by Eric D. Beinhocker, which talks about this concept.

To quickly summarize the book: the default future for the vast majority of companies, ultimately, is death. Companies die. But markets evolve and create innovations and are resilient. So I think by unleashing the power of Market-Based Dynamics within the organization, the chances of failure and ultimately the decline and death of the system is much, much lower than it would be in any traditional, hierarchal business structure.

It's a lot to process, and believe me, it's *been* a long process. But I'm also extremely optimistic that we've finally reached a tipping point.

Through DTP companies, I'm involved in some sizable construction projects here in Downtown Las Vegas, and I'm always fascinated by the way these construction projects go. It seems to take them two or three years during which it looks like nothing is happening, it's essentially an empty plot of land. They're running tests and digging the foundation and doing design work and getting permits and things, but it's just a dirt lot for two to three years. And then when they start building, suddenly it seems like it goes up overnight.

Another way I like to think of it is "linear growth" versus "exponential growth." Linear growth always beats exponential growth in the short term—until it doesn't. You can see it on a graph, when a nearly flat line that looks like it's going nowhere as it moves left to right suddenly shoots straight up into the air. It's also what happens with long-term compound interest in a retirement account.

Or you can use the classic example of pennies on a chessboard to describe this phenomenon. If given a choice, would you rather have a million pennies on each and every square of the chessboard (so 64 million pennies in total, or $640k), or one penny on the first square, two pennies on the second square, four pennies on the third square, and so on—keeping up that pattern of doubling the number of pennies in each square across the rest of the whole board?

Most people would choose the 64 million pennies. It's simple to see linear patterns, and it sounds like a lot of pennies. But the second choice is actually the smarter choice, financially speaking, because it's an exponential equation: By the time you reach the sixty-fourth square on the chess board, you will have accumulated 18,446,744,073,709,551,615 pennies. (Yes, those are commas. And yes, that is an unfathomably large number of pennies. As in more than the total number of grains of sand on the entire planet!)

I like the idea of exponential growth, and I'm hopeful that we're approaching that point on our long journey to self-organization.

If so, it could lead to a pretty disruptive change in the world of management science. Or maybe it's just our thing. Maybe no one else will care. But whenever there's massive disruptive change, most people don't even realize they're in the midst of it. It isn't until years later that people see it. Like the Wright brothers' first flight, for which they had no press or attention—not a single mention of their success, actually, until three years after the fact. How could man's first flight go basically unnoticed? For years? It seems impossible. Air travel would change everything about how we live and interact as humans. (This story is also referenced in a favorite book that we keep on hand in the Zappos library, Simon Sinek's *Start With Why*.)

Not that a self-organizing business model and structure is anything akin to man's first flight.

But if this works out the way it seems to be working out, I do believe there will be ripple effects from what we're doing here.

Amazon is interested. So are others. But Amazon gets the first peek, and they're watching closely because they realize that as they grow, in terms of people, that the hierarchical structure and top-down resource allocation methodology is not scaling with them. Their ability to make dynamic resource-allocation decisions has slowed, which happens in every hierarchical system at scale. Which means budgeting and other hierarchical decision-making processes don't scale, either.

Historically, the budgeting process at most sizable companies, including Zappos, has been done once a year, toward the end of each year, for the following year. But in real life, especially in the world we live in today, things change much faster than that—and there's no easy way to respond to changes in real time in a large organization.

What we're doing with CGB allows for a much faster response time.

Because the budgets are now in the hands of each individual circle, the budget adjustments can happen much like they would if you ran a bakery or any small business. You might come up with a general year-long plan, but if tomorrow you get twice as many customers, or half as many customers, you're going to adjust to that reality much faster than you would if you couldn't address the budget until the end of the year.

It's simple in concept: Smaller teams can individually make decisions much faster. But putting it into practice is a challenge, and we've really just begun to let that unfold, which is exciting.

Will other businesses do the same thing?

In the short term and medium term, it's hard to say. We're in a unique position in terms of our size, our deal with Amazon, our long-established culture and values. A company as large as Amazon or even half the size of Amazon can't experiment with dynamic resource allocation the way we can. But once we've established the framework and infrastructure and shown this model in practice, who knows?

With any luck, what we're doing here will inspire some new businesses to grow this type of self-organized system from the start, perhaps by leveraging our platform, instead of following the traditional hierarchical model from day one.

Tyler Williams
Head of Brand Aura
I married my high school sweetheart, Elissa, whom I started dating at age fourteen.

*In most companies, I think, doing nothing and just con-*tinuing business as usual is as dangerous as trying something radically new. Because eventually, if the average life span of most companies is fifteen years, you already know what's going to happen. To take no action means you're choosing the most likely scenario, which is to see your company end on a finite timeline. You're almost counting on the fact that at some point there's going to be a change you can't control, or you're just going to hit this obsolete point where the world changes around you.

So I find it strange and kind of baffling at times that so many companies are not willing to innovate at the same time they're doing whatever it is that has made them a success so far.

But enough about the structure. I want to talk about how exciting it is that it's actually here and that the possibility for so much to happen is right in front of us now.

For example, we recently took over what was previously known as the Axis Theater at Planet Hollywood. It's now called the Zappos Theater, and it's played host to concerts by the Backstreet Boys, Gwen Stefani, and Jennifer Lopez under our watch. There are probably plenty of people who think this is just one of those branding deals, like you find at stadiums all over America—where some big company pays big bucks to buy the naming rights to an already established or soon-to-be-built arena. But that's not the case here at all. We've actually set up a circle that's running the day-to-day merchandising operations for the Zappos Theater, and we're doing our best to infuse each concert experience with all of the service that Zappos is known for in conjunction with Caesar's.

We're looking to use technology and personal people skills to innovate the entire experience, from purchasing tickets to finding seats. We want to eliminate that big crush of people trying to buy concert merchandise before and after the show. Have you ever been stuck in one of those lines, which often turns into a bit of a mob scene, just trying to buy a t-shirt or a band-branded beer koozie after a show? It's terrible! A lot of people see that line and give up and walk away without the merchandise and memorabilia they want. We're trying to fix that, among other problems, all while we're getting new ideas from our concert-going customers. We're also working directly with some of the artists we host to design cool merchandise and make the experience better for *their* "customers," their fans, while we're at it.

And by sticking to our Zappos culture along the way, we can't help but make personal emotional connections (PECs) as we go.

Besides the theater, there are tons of creative ideas being thrown around as circles try to come up with ways to increase their profits both internally and externally, and I think some of the circles are going to come up with some really big ideas. Like, there could be a chain of Zappos Hotels, or Zappos Airlines, or who knows what, right? But those types of things, if anyone pursues them, will take a lot of time and funding to get off the ground. Which is why I think some of the most exciting stuff are the small ideas.

For example, there's a guy here who makes videos. Pat's his name, and he's basically a one-person circle at this point, and he bills around $5,000 a month internally—shooting videos for different circles who need videos. And he sometimes has

Daniel Oakley
Customer Loyalty Team, Social Media

In April 2018, Zappos Theater announced that it would be hosting Gwen Stefani's "Just a Girl" Las Vegas residency. Her fans went crazy on all of our social channels, especially on Twitter. I must have seen every Gwen GIF within thirty minutes of the announcement.

There were three fans who stuck out to me and were really engaging with our @ZapposTheater Twitter handle. While chatting with the three ladies (whom I lovingly refer to as "the queens"), I learned that they all lived in different cities in the United States and knew each other from attending Gwen concerts across the country. They would use the concerts as excuses to travel and meet up with each other. I probably talked to them for a good three hours the night of the residency announcement and was even invited to join their "ladies' night."

After conversing with them and building a bond, I just knew Zappos had to do something to give them that WOW experience! I sent the link of the Tweets thread to my lead, and we started on a game plan. We knew the dates the Gwen fans were coming out to Vegas, and they constantly kept in touch leading up to the residency's opening day. I was able to join them and I even wore a custom-made shirt that read "Honorary Queen." We WOWed these ladies with dinner before the show, gave them special goodie bags with memorabilia, and I got to rock out to Gwen with them in the pit! It was truly quite the experience and shows that a little PEC can go a long way.

downtime, such as when his videos are rendering on the computer. That's a time-consuming process and there's always downtime when he's just waiting for those videos to render. So he's been trying to come up with an income-generating business he could run during the downtime. It might be a very small business, but it doesn't matter. It would still be income-producing, which would raise the overall profit for his video circle and make it easier to balance his P&L.

He came up with a common thing that everyone needs: wiper blades. Most people drive to work here, and everybody needs their wiper blades replaced now and then. He knows how to change wiper blades and can do that out in the parking garage while he's waiting for things to render. It sounds so trivial, right? Until you get 1,500 people doing that same thing. Then essentially you have all of these mini-founders having that kind of founder mentality, like "Man, I've got to balance my P&L, so I need to find something people want, find customers, and then serve those customers."

So we could have grandiose ideas that would take a ton of funding to get off the ground, or we could have 1,500 employees all running side gigs and we accumulate all of that together. Or some combination of both, and a whole lot of in-between, which is the most likely scenario.

Let's say Pat just stays in-house, and he makes a profit of $5 per replacement. If he sells wipers to all 1,500 employees over the course of the year, that's $7,500.

Now what if all 1,500 employees are running little businesses that bring in an extra $7,500-a-year profit? That's $11.25 million. That's not insignificant.

The core business doesn't suffer, because these extra things can be done on the side. And then maybe, who knows, the wiper business starts finding external clients, and it becomes its own thing. And maybe he needs to hire someone else to help out, so he basically becomes CEO of the new Wiper Circle. And then he hires someone on the video side because now he's kind of splitting his time between the two. So it was one thing and then it divided, like a cell, or his little wiper baby business grew up. Maybe lots of people who work in Las Vegas want to take advantage of his wiper-replacement service and he grows it into a $10 million business. Why not? Stranger things have happened, right?

And not everyone has to be an entrepreneur for this to work. The only entrepreneur in the local bakery is the owner of the bakery, right? So if Pat the video guy is the entrepreneur, his employees in the video business and the wiper business can just do their jobs, editing video and replacing wipers. But if they *do* have an entrepreneurial spirit, they'll have the ability to hire themselves out to other circles and start up their own new initiatives as well. And we'll support them in that. So it never ends. We could truly have a building full of 500 thriving start-ups at any one time, generating budget-related income within the building by providing services to other circles—like, hypothetically, maybe the Wiper Circle needs a wiper scheduling website to be created by our Digital Customer Experience circle—or generating external income, the way one of the circles I oversee, which used to produce parties internally complete with sound, lights, set up, tear down, and so on, now sells its services to businesses all over town. It's turned into a great little business, and it's growing fast, because we have a platform of throwing our own Zappos parties that now become a showcase for our product, which we can sell to the vendors and others who experience our parties!

Like I said, it never ends. The possibilities just grow and grow.

Another example: Miguel, our resident artist, has started a business at Zappos now. Originally it started just as him getting funded for his unique job, doing what he loves, just for Zappos. But the folks at Amazon have always admired his work, and one day we took him up for some meetings at Amazon and they were like, "Why can't Miguel do a mural right there?" So we lent him out to do a mural for them and they said, "Can we just keep him?

We want him to do murals everywhere." Our response was, "No, he's ours. You can't keep him. But . . . do you want to look over his menu of services?"

Amazon didn't hesitate to pay thousands of dollars for one of his mural projects. He realized he could bring in additional money from other companies that want his services, too. And he's in the process of turning it into a full business now, talking about hiring other artists, maybe a whole team of artists.

Miguel Hernandez
Art Curator and Creative

Yeah! I'm working to get the funding for one more resident artist right now, and then, who knows? I'd like to build a whole army of artists. We could add artwork to offices all over the place. I'm so busy, I really do need another set of hands. And I can "Do More with Less," but I also can do more with more. I think we can really build this into something special. I'm in the process of running the numbers and putting a whole plan together. And again, I never imagined myself being an entrepreneur or heading up a team of artists. I never imagined I'd curate an art show, either, but I've done that now. I've done a lot of things because of Zappos and the way this place works. And there's so much more to come!

Chris Mattice
Finance
I quit my previous job in 2010 to become a professional poker player.

We are even designing a new end-to-end financial system called the CFO Tool. Its thirty-second pitch is that it's "hands-off-the-wheel budgeting" for employees, like Miguel, who have never envisioned themselves as traditional managers but find themselves creating a new business. It's a system that will allow Customer-Generated Budgeting to work smoothly by empowering lead links to manage their own budgets with ease.

Our goal at the beginning of the project was to deliver WOW to our internal customers, create transparency, and make it available 24/7 (like our amazing CLT reps). It also had to be intuitive to use. Next, we assembled a great team of engineers and visual designers to build the CFO Tool, making it clear and simple for everyone, even if this new process seems scary. We completed exhaustive user testing and asked, "What are the top things you love and hate most about our current systems?" The feedback was pretty amazing. Early on, Tyler Williams told me he would pay my circle $100,000 if he never had to log in to the system we were using and approve a purchase order again, so we went to the drawing board and made it happen.

Imagine, in the future, a system that combines everything a small (or even large) business uses—enterprise resource planning, treasury, recruiting, human resources, payroll, purchasing, inventory, accounts payable, accounts receivable, and reporting—into one online tool. The result would be something that has never been created before. But we wanted to provide this great service to everyone at Zappos so lead links who may not have ever been a manager before can run with a project and manage their circle's finances like a seasoned pro.

With the CFO Tool lead links can make decisions without approval from a senior leader or finance. If a lead link decides they need to change direction or allocate their budget differently, that's fine. The lead link can update their budget in the CFO Tool at any time since it's all online. It connects multiple systems across the organization, enabling lead links to do "one-stop shopping" for most of their needs. The CFO Tool also has a lot of ad-hoc reporting built in so finance can still get what they need as well. I think the coolest thing is the transparency we have built into the CFO Tool, and every employee at Zappos is able to see the finances of every other circle.

Here is the vision for the CFO Tool and how it will support Customer-Generated Budgeting and Market-Based Dynamics: Customer-Generated Budgeting involves setting up service agreements between lead links of different circles as service providers and as customers. The service agreements are designed to make implicit work explicit and help facilitate expectations for the circles so there are no surprises and both sides can hold each other accountable. Revenue is earned monthly by the service provider circle and paid via internal invoicing in the CFO Tool from the customer circle. A circle can also earn revenue from completing bounties, invoicing ad-hoc work completed for their customers, or by generating additional external revenue. This eliminates the annualized budgeting process and changes the process for a lead link to be as simple as balancing your checkbook. Just like in the real world for each of our employees' daily lives, as long as your bank balance does not go negative, everything is good.

Tia Zuniga

Experimental Marketing and Brand Strategy

I broke my arm every year of elementary school. A combination of being clumsy, adventurous, and not liking to be told what to do.

*There's another incentive to moving toward self-orga-*nization: Flipping the traditional managerial pyramid on its head, letting your people take the wheel—that actually takes a lot of the pressure off a CEO and allows him or her to do the things that they're really passionate about. The things they're *great* at.

> *"You're so vain . . . I bet you think this song is about you . . . Don't you? Don't you?" . . . Just kidding, I really think Tia's talking about me like I'm not here.*
>
> TONY

I don't think it's a secret that a lot of start-up CEOs don't like the more traditional roles they're forced to take on once their company is at scale. The self-organization model changes that. It frees someone like Tony to do the things he's passionate about while letting others who are passionate about other aspects of the business tackle those challenges. It's like the biggest form of delegating, ever. Turn it over to your employees. Let them take the lead on projects. Once you get the right people who are the right culture fit and company fit, and you're confident that you're all moving in the same direction, self-organization lets those people be great! It's not outsourcing the work or not doing your job. It's getting those people who are going to be passionate about that part of it that you *aren't* passionate about to lend their talents to those areas. It just makes sense.

Case in point: After Tony wrote *Delivering Happiness*, he didn't want to write a follow-up book. Publishers asked him about it. Friends asked him about it. Other business leaders asked him about it. He just wasn't interested. Not that he didn't think we were doing plenty of interesting things at Zappos. He just wasn't interested in being known as an author and wasn't interested at all in making it all about himself.

So my team stepped in.

Not to get too meta here, but that in and of itself is a very Zapponian story. After Kelly Smith (our lead link) and her fiancée (whom she met and started dating here at Zappos), Derrin Hawkins, and I formed a circle (as part of an employee contest meant to encourage us to embrace the cross-cultivation of self-organization), we came up with this out-of-the-box idea of letting our *employees* write a book. We found budgeting for it through the marketing department and Brand Aura, and we did some research, finding a *New York Times*–bestselling writer who fell in love with our culture and our desire to inspire, whom we knew we could trust to help us put it all together. We hired an agent and fielded interest from some large publishers, and in the end we chose to go with BenBella, a smaller publisher out of Texas with whom we just vibed, in the most Zappos way possible—because they made us an offer that felt like it was truly in service to us, as well as to our potential readers.

So this very book that you're holding in your hands is a direct result of self-organization and MBD and the wonders of self-organization in action!

Looking around here at some of the other ideas that have already risen to the surface, it makes me think of the reality show *Undercover Boss*. The premise is that the CEOs of some pretty big companies put on wigs and prosthetic noses and Clark Kent–style glasses to disguise themselves so they can go "under-cover" and get hired in lower positions in their own companies. It gives them a chance to experience what's happening on the front lines, at the restaurant counter or in the shipping bay or with the janitorial staff. In their disguises they have the freedom to talk to their workers with complete openness and honesty, and some of these bosses actually uncover things that they never knew about their own companies. Problems that need fixing, sure. But they also discover incredibly talented, forward-thinking individuals way down at the bottom of the traditional pyramid. And then, for the sake of making good television, they reveal themselves in a dramatic scene, and the people are always shocked. Then the CEO rewards those workers for their good ideas, sometimes promoting them to higher positions or giving them bonuses, and implementing some of their ideas to make the company better.

My questions is: Why does that need to be done undercover? What if *all* CEOs did this out in the open, all the time? We all laugh about it because I'm not sure that Tony could go under-cover. We all know him too well. A disguise wouldn't work.

I'm not sure this is completely true. This reminds me of the time when I was in seventh grade and entered our middle school's Halloween contest. I put on makeup and a wig and my mom's clothes. The teachers lined up all the contestants, including myself, against the wall. I found out later that they had disqualified me, because one of the judges looked at me and said, "What is she dressed up as?!"

We see him all the time. We email him with questions, and he answers. We ask for a meeting, and he meets with us (although sometimes it may take a couple of weeks to get on his calendar).

But to the CEOs who don't work that way, I assume you wouldn't keep your workforce around if you didn't think they

> *Empower your employees, and the results can be astounding.*

were pretty smart, right? Pretty good at what they do? So why not tap into those brilliant minds all around you and let them help you move your company forward, right now, instead of waiting and reacting to the inevitable changes in the marketplace that your people on the ground probably already see coming?

It takes more than just listening, though, even though listening is a really good start! It takes the trust of giving them the power to make changes.

Empower your employees, and the results can be astounding.

Chris Peake
Strategic Initiatives
I'm a runner, but I run because I like drinking beer, not because I like running ☺

We've seen some really great individual successes so far under self-organization and our evolving system of self-management. But the more Market-Based Dynamics comes into its own, the more I firmly believe it's going to magnify our success rate ten times.

Managers make a lot of good decisions, but traditional leadership alone will never make the right decisions *all* the time. To echo Tia: You need to listen to people that are on the ground, the forces directly talking to your customers about what their needs are. Then? Give those people the actual keys to the car, and let them drive it around.

The more empowered your people are, the more innovative they will become. And ultimately, once they feel they're truly in the driver's seat, that's when the most amazing, disruptive, innovative ideas are going to pop up.

Tyler Williams
Head of Brand Aura
I built a Flame Defense Roomba-Powered Beer Pong Table.

It's been a long time coming. And we went super slow, specifically with MBD, because we wanted to get this right. And the biggest slowdown of all, honestly, the biggest hindrance we've dealt with, is just the psychological fear of what MBD and CGB might require in terms of accountability.

As much as people complain about it, there is a small minority of people who are so used to hiding behind the lack of accountability in the old systems of budgeting and management that they are truly scared of what might happen when those old walls of separation disappear.

Well, that time is now, and most people here at Zappos have finally reached a point of thinking, "Okay. I can handle this."

Once we settle into it, I'm guessing it will be as positive an experience as our move to Downtown LV has become for most people now. The hesitation and fear are just natural responses that take time to overcome, I guess.

But now that it's all coming into place, I think things are going to move a lot faster.

It's not theoretical anymore.

It's real.

I know there are a lot of skeptics out there. I know because I meet them. Most of the world is so entrenched in the typical hierarchy that people aren't afraid to share their doubts about what we're doing, right out in the open.

"You really think this will work?"

"Is this really possible?"

"There's just no way you'll see enough positive cash flow come out of these 'side' endeavors to make it worthwhile. I mean, come on!"

"All this self-organization crap is gonna kill your core business!"

Selling a little swag on the side might seem like small potatoes. (It's not.) The profits that could be made from one talented employee painting murals might seem small, too, right? Maybe even inconsequential in the big scheme of corporate profits— although it's clearly not inconsequential to Miguel, and it's not inconsequential to any of us who live surrounded by his beautiful artwork every day.

But I understand what people are thinking: "Even if a whole bunch of these ideas take off and we have dozens, even hundreds, of teams bringing in new profits, it will take years to see the results of all this experimentation. So why even bother?"

Well, guess what? It hasn't taken years. We're already seeing results.

Real results.

WOW-worthy, *profitable* results that are a true win-win for all involved.

Of course, we're not going to reveal everything in this book. After all, we're just getting started. We'll have plenty more stories to tell as we head into our next two decades, let alone our next two *centuries*.

But what you're about to see in the next chapter is just one example of what can happen when everything we've talked about in this book comes together, all at once.

And the results are anything but "small potatoes."

THE POWER OF
ZAPPOS ADAPTIVE

Saul Dave
Enterprise Systems

I am an adrenaline junkie. I have done the world's highest bungee jump, a 14,500-foot tandem skydive, cage dived with great white sharks, and flew in a Red Bull aerobatic plane in a full aerobatic performance. I also am incredibly accident prone and hurt myself all the time . . . not the best combo.

It all started with a phone call.

I was going through new-hire training in July 2014 when I took a call from a customer named Tonya who had received the wrong size shoes.

The shoes that Tonya ordered were adult-sized sneakers that closed with hook and loop instead of traditional shoelaces.

I apologized for sending the wrong size and tried to replace them for her. But I couldn't. The size she wanted simply wasn't available, and despite my search efforts on our website I couldn't find a similar replacement.

When I shared the news with Tonya she seemed rather exasperated and sad.

Sensing that she was disappointed, I asked her why, hoping I could make it up to her. She shared that the shoes were for her grandson, Gabriel, who has autism, and who was unable to tie his shoelaces. Apparently, his fine motor skills never developed in a way that allowed him to master that task. When he was small, it wasn't a big deal since many manufacturers made kids' shoes with hook and loop closure. Now that he was getting older and his body was growing, it became more difficult to find cool-looking athletic shoes without laces.

"Wow," I said. "I had no idea that was something that was so difficult to find."

"Yes," Tonya said. "That's why I was so excited to find them on Zappos, and I'm so disappointed now. I just don't know what he's going to do. This is so frustrating for him."

"Look," I said, "I'm going to put some notes down here and see what we can do, okay? If I can find you these shoes anywhere else, anywhere else at *all*, I'll call you back. In the meantime, go ahead and keep the shoes we sent."

"But they won't fit," she said.

"I know. But there's no need to return them. You can go ahead and give them to someone who can use them. Maybe donate them to an organization that helps others like your grandson. No charge. We'll refund your money."

"Really?" she said.

"I already processed your refund while we were talking."

"That's wonderful. Thank you!"

After the call I looked for another retailer or even a shoe company that made fashionable, attractive adult footwear that might be right for Gabriel, but I had no luck. None at all. It quickly became obvious to me that there wasn't an online company that specialized in shoes and clothing for people who had similar needs as Gabriel.

I was completely unaware of the needs and challenges that people with autism faced in general. And I surely wasn't familiar with the challenges they faced getting dressed. I had no personal connection to the obvious frustration and sadness Tonya expressed on the phone. I just knew she needed help. Her need sparked my thinking: *There must be many other customers just like her who are struggling to find the kinds of shoes and clothing their family members need.*

As I started to search for shoes that were easier to put on, initially I found some orthotic shoes sold on medical supply sites, which left a lot to be desired because they were not stylish. The shoes and clothes I managed to find were functional for specific needs, or looked like they were designed for older people. There was a real void in terms of combining fashion with functional clothing and shoes. This gap in the market-place made me wonder if Zappos could create a category on our website just to serve that "adaptive" market. I brought it up with a few of our executives, and they all said, "That sounds like a good idea!"

The intention didn't initially translate to action, though. Nothing happened for months.

That's pretty typical in the flurry of trying to keep up with the daily needs of a thriving company, isn't it? A lot of ideas don't get past the idea stage.

As we went through the changeover to self-organization and the Teal Offer, my thoughts about the adaptive category faded into the background—until, almost as if by fate, the following summer one of my contacts at the software company SAP invited me to attend an "Els for Autism" charity golf event. Ernie Els, the professional golfer from South Africa, has a son

> *It was the first time I fully understood how moving to a self-managed organizational model could be a really positive thing. I didn't have to answer to someone "higher up." I was free to pursue the idea on my own.*

with autism, and SAP supports his foundation. So I went to this event and met a lot of incredible people, and I listened to a presentation that outlined how SAP has committed to hiring people with autism to fill 1 percent of their workforce. This stoked the fire in me to revisit how Zappos could introduce adaptive clothing and shoes for people with disabilities.

Around that same time, I noticed a lot of press reports about the high incidence of children diagnosed with autism—which turns out to be one in fifty-nine. I interpreted that data to mean that a substantial number of families in America must be affected by this. And yet, most retailers seemed to be slow to respond to the needs of these kids and their parents, not to mention the millions of adults who could benefit from shoes and clothing designed or adapted more specifically to their individual needs.

At Zappos I spoke to Scott Schaefer—one of our executives in finance—to see if I could get permission to explore the opportunity in the adaptive space. I said, "Scott, we need to do something. There's a huge need for this." And he said, "Just go ahead and do it. You don't need anybody's permission anymore."

It was the first time I fully understood how moving to a self-managed organizational model could be a really positive thing. I didn't have to answer to someone "higher up." I was free to pursue the idea on my own.

So I did.

I started sending out emails to various groups within Zappos, from marketing to buyers to Brand Aura, which was dedicated entirely to elevating the brand through all sorts of innovative means, and, slowly but surely, I put together a small team of people who believed in the vision I had. We didn't know exactly what we wanted to do, and we certainly didn't have any road map to follow when it came to figuring out how to do it—I mean, if one dedicated grandmother struggled to the point of tears trying to find a single pair of stylish sneakers without laces for her growing grandson, how on earth were we going to source enough product to fill a whole adaptive category?

That challenge was exacerbated because it took time to find the right team here at Zappos, with the right mix of skill sets and backgrounds, to pull this together. Early on, Dana Zumbo came on board. She has an extensive background in merchandising and had spent most of her life doing volunteer work with children and adults with disabilities. We also needed a fashion buyer, and Derek Flores joined to help source product. Eventually Molly Kettle joined the team as director of Zappos Adaptive, bringing experience with both websites and running cross-functional teams. Over the course of 2016 into early 2017, this small team got things rolling.

"We put together PowerPoints and business plans," Molly recalls.

"We pitched all over the building," adds Dana.

Our focus expanded from initially trying to meet the needs of people with autism to buying shoes and clothes to make life easier for anyone who needs adaptations to clothes to allow them to dress independently and with confidence. We did extensive research to learn about those needs by talking with and getting feedback from people with disabilities, parents of children with disabilities, customers, and organizations that serve people with disabilities.

The pitches went well, and we were able to secure some funding from within the company to get us started. We officially launched the Zappos Adaptive site in April 2017 with just two new brands, and—based on our understanding of the various needs—we were able to curate some clothing and shoes that were already for sale on the Zappos website.

Then we focused on grassroots marketing to spread the word, and that was when something magical happened: We caught the attention of Nike. Yes, *Nike*!

Let me explain. Because of her experience working with families touched by autism, Dana knew about the Nike FlyEase—a great example of how Nike innovates on behalf of athletes of all abilities. Nike FlyEase allows someone to drop their foot in the shoe and go without the fuss of shoelaces. It works for all kinds of needs.

After we launched Zappos Adaptive, Dana reached out to Aaron Triche, the Zappos buyer who oversees the Nike partnership. The timing was perfect—Aaron let Dana know that the Nike team would in the office in the next few days and invited Dana to attend the meeting to share the Zappos Adaptive story.

Little did we know that at the same time Dana had reached out to Aaron, Nike had also reached out to Zappos Adaptive. As it turns out, Nike had learned about Zappos Adaptive from a Facebook post that hit close to home for an employee whose nephew has autism. This employee had shared the post with her sister and asked her to share with her network of moms.

As she tells the story, "I thought of my sister and her family, the adjustments and sacrifices they've had to make for their son and thought—this could be one less thing to worry about. Finding shoes that are easy to get on and off and clothes that limit sensory overload (that look good, too, by the way)—on one site? And by an amazing service company like Zappos? More people need to know, and Nike needs to be a part of it!"

Dana then asked, "So how do we get the Nike FlyEase product on the Zappos Adaptive website?"

This is a big deal because, at that point in time, Nike.com was the only place you could get FlyEase. No other retailers carried it.

Less than two months after the initial meeting with Nike, we received an email from Nike stating that the company was excited to share that Zappos Adaptive will be able to offer the FlyEase product starting in spring 2018. And that the launch of the Adaptive site was a catalyst to this distribution change.

Nike believed in our mission and it aligns with Nike's mission to serve athletes of all abilities. We have since forged a close partnership with the Nike team and have touched the lives of tens of thousands of customers who can now wear their favorite Nike shoes with ease, style, and uncompromised performance.

Having a brand like Nike as a partner is huge. We love what they're doing, and having the FlyEase available on our website has helped to put adaptive fashion on the map and Zappos grow and change the lives of more people.

For Nike, they shared that it wasn't about business but about doing the right thing.

Around the same time, we met a fascinating innovator and entrepreneur named Billy Price. Back when he was an engineering student in college, Billy fell out of a three-story building. He broke his neck, resulting in quadriplegia, which left him with limited arm and hand mobility. As an engineering student, Billy was used to being able to solve hard problems and come up with clever solutions. So after his accident, he was able to figure out a lot of things for himself: He went back to school, finished his degree, and remastered how to drive a car. He was even able to figure out tricks to help him get dressed.

But one problem always persisted: being able to put on his shoes. Slipping on shoes was difficult, and tying them was almost impossible.

Billy and his longtime friend Darin Donaldson ultimately developed a shoe design that redefined how to get shoes easily on and off. The shoes have a zipper function that opens from one side of the shoe all the way around the front toe, and the upper flips up and folds over to open completely, like a book.

For Billy, this universal design makes it easy to put his foot straight in from the top, unobstructed, rather than jamming his foot in. And the best part is that Billy and his team made the shoes super stylish so anyone would want to wear them. As the BILLY Footwear slogan says: "Universal design with fashion in mind!"

We started selling Billy's shoes on our site, and everything has just continued to grow from there.

Today we offer a broad assortment of easy-on/off shoes, plus sensory-friendly clothing, reversible shirts and pants, clothing with magnetic fasteners (for those who have a hard time buttoning traditional buttons), postsurgical clothing, diabetic shoes, compression gear, and more.

"It's been so important to listen to customers and other advisers in this space along the way," Dana notes. "We've spoken with parents and grandparents, like Tonya, people with disabilities, friends and family right here in our own Zappos family about what their needs are, and we continue to work toward filling those needs with the product we offer. We also had people from the local physical and occupational therapy communities reach out to us."

Based on this outreach, and as a way to learn faster and solicit feedback, we hosted an event for the local community on our campus. One jewel of insight that came out of that night was the suggestion that we ought to attend national conferences where OTs and PTs gather, since they are on the front line serving people with disabilities and their families. These OTs and PTs understand, recommend, and create solutions to make life easier for their clients.

"We decided to attend a national PT conference in February 2018 to see if it made sense for us to host a booth at future conferences," Molly recalls. "We noticed that there was very little representation of any clothing or footwear among the exhibitors at the conference, so we made the decision to exhibit at the national OT conference in April 2018. It opened up so many conversations with the occupational therapy community."

We learned that OTs help their clients find shoes that fit over certain orthotics, work around certain mobility issues, and provide easy-on/off capabilities for wheelchair users. The OTs also shared that the solutions they create aren't being mass-produced or made available for purchase. It seemed that everyone who needed something adapted for a particular need was going back to the drawing board and starting from scratch. The OTs were very excited to hear about the products we curated from vendors and were surprised to see that some of the solutions they created on a case-by-case basis were now being mass-produced by some brands.

"The best part of all, though," Molly says, "is seeing the impact it has on people when they realize there are options available to them that will meet their needs. We have hosted a booth in both Houston and LA at the Abilities Expo, which is a consumer-facing show. We met many, many people who often get emotional (and we do, too!) when their children try on shoes that not only fit their braces but look cute. Or when a man who has struggled with shoes his whole life realizes the Nike FlyEase will make putting his shoes on ten times easier. Or when a woman, who is a wheelchair user, realizes she can wear jeans after she couldn't find a pair that would work for her for twenty years.

"People share with us their stories about the challenges they have," Molly continues. "The idea that they could go online and buy shoes and clothing that their kids won't struggle with, that they could alleviate some of the frustrations they feel on a daily basis—that is why we do what we do."

We created an advisory council to provide input, expertise, and insight to Zappos Adaptive on a regular basis. We sought those with experience in this space, who share the goal of helping to make life easier for people with disabilities who don't want to compromise fashion for function. The members of our council are a diverse group, which includes business owners, fashion consultants, marketing consultants, organization leaders, a Miss America contestant, Boston Marathon bombing survivors, and the founder of the Runway of Dreams Foundation (RoDF).

As part of our initial research, we found out about RoDF, whose mission centers around promoting inclusion of people with disabilities in the fashion industry. We reached out to founder Mindy Scheier and had our first conversation over lunch in New York in 2017, just before we launched our website. We immediately felt connected, as Mindy shared her personal story about her son who has a rare form of muscular dystrophy and has difficulty getting dressed. Based on her professional experience as a fashion designer, she saw an opportunity to be a disruptor in the fashion industry through inclusion.

Each year, RoDF hosts a gala and fashion show that show-cases models with disabilities, and the event raises funds for its programming. Mindy invited us to attend in 2017 and we attended again in 2018, this time as honorees to receive an inclusivity award. We then went on to collaborate with Mindy and her team to host a Zappos Adaptive and Runway of Dreams fashion show in Las Vegas in March 2019. We outfitted thirty models with disabilities in a range of adaptive clothing and footwear, and they walked the runway in front of a crowd of more than 1,000. It was an incredible experience!

Through RoDF we met several senior leaders from Tommy Hilfiger and PVH. Tommy Hilfiger has been a pioneer in adaptive clothing by modifying its existing men's, women's, and kids' classic clothing with adaptations—or, as they call them, "hidden innovations"—that make getting dressed easier. Derek Flores, our team member who is a buyer for Zappos Adaptive, began conversations with Tommy prior to the 2017 RoDF gala event, and through Mindy's connections and our growing relationship with the brand, we began carrying the Tommy Adaptive line in late 2018.

"We also have a great story about a specific shoe from Converse," Molly says. "Converse made a slip-on shoe with a hook-and-loop back that folds open called the Easy Slip, and we'd heard from a lot of parents with kids wearing AFOs—that's ankle-foot orthosis, or braces on their legs to assist them in walking—that the Easy Slip shoe worked for them. We highlighted the shoe on Zappos Adaptive when we first launched. But then we noticed that the inventory on the Easy Slip kept dropping. We were running out of sizes, so we reached out to our buyer, Kara, and she told us, 'Yes, I know about the inventory levels because it's being discontinued.'"

All of this good we're doing—putting everything Zappos stands for into action—isn't just good for the world. It's good for business.

We simply didn't want that to happen, so Dana met with Kara, who set us up with a call with Converse. We put together a plan and shared with them how important these shoes were to many of our customers. Converse agreed to add the Easy Slip back into production, exclusively to sell on the Zappos Adaptive website!

"It's stories like this that keep us motivated," Dana says. "Stories that I don't think could ever happen if it weren't for the freedom we've had to explore this opportunity, on our own, and to work in partnership with so many teams within Zappos, and all around us in the community, to accomplish our mission."

Throughout this whole experience, we truly have felt like we have been running our own start-up within the larger Zappos company. As a start-up, we are very cautious and intentional about our spend, we analyze opportunities for potential return on investment, and we do more with less at every turn. Yet, what's really exciting is that all of this good we're doing—putting everything Zappos stands for into action, all at once—isn't just good for the world. It's good for business.

In our first full year up and running, Zappos Adaptive posted millions of dollars in sales—yes, millions—almost entirely through word-of-mouth and grassroots marketing, driven by the power of partnering with brands and communities who care about people. We've been successful because of the input from our external advisers and support from folks right here on campus. We work with teams who do website design, marketing, creative, PR, legal, finance, merchandising, audio/visual, and more, who have all been wholly committed to seeing Zappos Adaptive succeed. We truly cherish our relationships with the different teams, and we work hard to be great partners, internally as well as externally.

> *Our goal is service—to make it easier for customers who need these products to find them. We want to impact lives, and we've found that accomplishing that great big goal can be as simple as giving our customers options that help make getting dressed easier.*

Initially our small team began with just a few people wearing a lot of hats. Molly and Dana started our Zappos Adaptive Facebook page, which we quickly recognized as a great channel for reaching the communities and people we were trying to serve. As it grew, we wanted to take on more and have a presence on other platforms, so we decided to add a social media manager. In April 2018, we brought on Lori Wong, who had experience working at Zappos in the photo studio. An accomplished photographer, she has been a wonderful addition to the team, creating and managing @ZapposAdaptive on Facebook, Instagram, and Twitter.

It's all growing so fast, it's difficult to predict how big this could get. To be honest, profiting from the creation of what is essentially a new market wasn't our goal. Not at all. Our goal is service—to make it easier for customers who need these products to find them. We want to impact lives, and we've found that accomplishing that great big goal can be as simple as giving our customers options that help make getting dressed easier.

In the three years between talking to Tonya and finally launching Zappos Adaptive, I tried to call Tonya back on dozens of occasions. I wanted to let her know what that conversation from so long ago had sparked and inspired. But she never picked up the phone.

Finally, one day in late 2017, our team was sitting in a conference room when we were brainstorming how to communicate about Zappos Adaptive from an authentic point of view. We decided to try and call Tonya one more time.

Miraculously, Tonya picked up.

"I was just making dinner," she said. "I thought you were a telemarketer! But I had seen this same number so many times, I thought, 'I'll just see who it is.'"

I said, "This is Saul from Zappos. Do you remember that call from a few years ago about the shoes for your grandson?" I told her the whole story of what her call had inspired, and she was speechless.

"I can't believe that there's a company out there that cares," she said. "Thank you so much for what you're doing—not only for Gabriel, but for all kinds of kids who need shoes without laces or clothes that make it easier to get dressed."

Tonya lived in Atlanta and had never been to Las Vegas. So we flew her out.

"She met the whole team and a lot of other Zappos people," Molly says.

"We took her out on the town," Dana recalls.

We just wanted her to know how much we appreciated her and to know that she was part of the family now. Today, she follows us on Facebook to stay up-to-date on what we are doing.

It's hard to explain to people what it feels like to create something like this, and to do it within the walls of this company, knowing that none of us came here for this particular purpose at the beginning.

"My entire career has been in retail merchandising," Dana says. "But I was involved in Special Olympics as a volunteer before I came to Zappos. I worked with kids with autism, teaching swimming and recreation on the side, and now we're close to the autism community here in a different way through our work, and it's awesome. To be able to be here on this team that sells products for people in a community that I served for so long, how does that even happen? There's no way I ever thought that I could bring my passion for retail and my love of working with kids and adults together in a job that is so fulfilling. I'm the luckiest person in the world. That's how I feel."

> *I go home and I work, and over the weekend I work, and we travel and I work, but it's not like work. I know what work feels like, and this isn't the same.*

"I feel that way, too," Molly says. "It's the perfect storm. A perfect role—I feel like my past work experiences have prepared me for this. All of us are so fulfilled and it doesn't even feel like 'work.'"

"Right?" Dana says. "I go home and I *work*, and over the weekend I *work*, and we travel and I *work*, but it's not like work. I know what work feels like, and this isn't the same."

Molly agrees. "At the end of the day, I'm always saying, 'Can I have another day in the week? Because I need to get more done!'

I honestly don't remember what it's like to watch the clock and think, 'Can I go home now?'"

"It's really hard to put into words sometimes," Dana says.

"We're just grateful," Molly adds.

What drives the team to do this work can be summed up in an experience at a recent Abilities Expo in Houston. Between 6,000 and 7,000 people came through over the course of the weekend, and at one point Molly looked over at Dana and noticed she was standing next to a young woman in a wheelchair who was crying. When they asked her why she was crying after trying on a pair of Nike FlyEase shoes over her leg braces, she looked up with tears on her face and said, "I've never been able to buy shoes that fit like this. It's—oh my goodness. Wow! I'm just . . . *Wow!*"

This young woman was twenty-nine years old, and had struggled for a very long time to find shoes that worked for her.

"She came back the next day and was showing everyone who walked by," Molly says. "She was saying, 'You've got to come see this. Come look!' We had moms come over with their children to try on shoes. I began crying with these mothers because they found something that makes a real impact in their lives. In this job, we're crying all the time."

"When you see the impact firsthand, that just keeps you going," Dana adds. "Because you're not just helping one person. You know, it's a matter of 'Help one, and you help many.'"

I would say that pretty much sums up everything we've tried to do here at Zappos Adaptive, and everything we've tried to share here in this book. Help one, help many.

What a great way to work.

What a great way to *live*.

AFTERWORD

One of my favorite quotes is "A great brand is a story that never stops unfolding."

I think the same is true for a company, for a community, and for a city.

That's why I'm so excited to be a resident of Downtown Las Vegas right now,

and that's why I'm so excited to be part of the next stage of the Zappos adventure.

I can't wait to see what unfolds next.

Tony

Are you feeling adventurous?

Follow this code to see what unfolds…
You never know where it might lead:

For more stories, resources, surprises, and shopping,
please visit us at zappospowerofwow.com

Feeling social or want to chat?

Call us 24/7
877-927-2332

Is your thinking cap on?

Let's try something fun together.
As we continue to evolve, we need your help.

Please fill in the blank:

We are a service company that
happens to _____.

We would love some inspiration for our next adventure.
Will Zappos go to the moon? Will Zappos invent something crazy?

Email us your suggestions at powerofwow@zappos.com or cut this
section out and mail us your answer for a special surprise:

Zappos Power of Wow
400 Stewart Avenue
Las Vegas, NV 89101

THE OATH OF EMPLOYMENT

No. 1. Deliver WOW Through Service

At Zappos, anything worth doing is worth doing with WOW. WOW is such a short, simple word, but it really encompasses a lot of things.

To WOW, you must differentiate yourself, which means doing something a little unconventional and innovative. You must WOW (go above and beyond what's expected) in every interaction with coworkers, vendors, customers, the community, investors—with everyone. And whatever you do must have an emotional impact on the receiver.

We are not an average company, our service is not average, and we don't want our people to be average. We expect every employee to deliver WOW. Whether internally with coworkers or externally with our customers and partners, delivering WOW results in word of mouth.

Our philosophy at Zappos is to WOW with service and experience, not with anything that relates directly to monetary compensation (for example, we don't offer blanket discounts or promotions to customers). We seek to WOW our customers, our coworkers, our vendors, our partners, and, in the long run, our investors.

Ask Yourself: What are things you can improve upon in your work or attitude to WOW more people? Have you WOWed at least one person today?

* Helps even when it "isn't their job." It's fine to take individual action until there is a chance to bring an expectation to a governance meeting.
* WOWs everyone, everywhere.
* Actually makes someone say "WOW."
* Frames interactions to elicit the most positive outcome for the customer while keeping in mind Zappos' best interests. Customer = someone shopping on the site, vendors, coworkers, candidates, EVERYONE.

No. 2. Embrace and Drive Change

Part of being in a growing company is that change is constant. For some people, especially those who come from bigger companies, the constant change can be somewhat unsettling at first. If you are not prepared to deal with constant change, then you probably are not a good fit for the company.

We must all learn not only to not fear change but to embrace it enthusiastically and, perhaps even more importantly, to encourage and drive it. We must always plan for and be prepared for constant change. Change can and will come from all directions. It's important that anyone, anywhere in the organization, is a sensor for meaningful change. Especially and including roles that are closest to our customers and/or issues.

Never accept or be too comfortable with the status quo, because historically, the companies that get into trouble are the ones that aren't able to respond quickly enough and adapt to change. We are ever evolving. If we want to continue to stay ahead of our competition, we must continually change and keep them guessing. They can copy our images, our shipping, and the overall look of our website, but they cannot copy our people, our culture, or our service. And they will not be able to evolve as fast as we can as long as embracing constant change is a part of our culture.

Ask Yourself: How do you plan and prepare for change? Do you view new challenges optimistically? Do you encourage and drive change? How do you encourage more change to be driven from all areas of the organization? Are you empowering your fellow circle members to process their tensions, improve the structure of their circles by bringing issues to governance meetings, and drive change?

Sample Behaviors for This Value

* Drives original thinking.
* Challenges the status quo or common wisdom.
* Is comfortable with chaos.
* Experiments with new ideas before going all in. Bullets versus cannonballs.

No. 3. Create Fun and a Little Weirdness

One of the things that makes Zappos different from a lot of other companies is that we value being fun and being a little weird. We don't want to become one of those big companies that feels corporate and boring. We want to be able to laugh at ourselves. We look for both fun and humor in our daily work. This means that many things we do might be a little unconventional—or else it wouldn't be a little weird.

We're not looking for crazy or extreme weirdness, though. We want just a touch of weirdness to make life more interesting and fun for everyone. We want the company to have a unique and memorable personality. Our company culture is what makes us successful, and in our culture we celebrate and embrace our diversity and each person's individuality. We want people to express their personality in their work. To outsiders, that might come across as inconsistent or weird. But the consistency is in our belief that we function best when we can be ourselves. We want the weirdness in each of us to be expressed in our interactions with each other and in our work.

One of the side effects of encouraging weirdness is that it encourages people to think outside the box and be more innovative. When you combine a little weirdness with making sure everyone is also having fun at work, it ends up being a win-win for everyone: Employees are more engaged in the work that they do, and the company as a whole becomes more innovative.

Ask Yourself: What can we do to be a little weird and differentiate ourselves from everyone else? What can we do that's both fun and a little weird? How much fun do you have in your job, and what can you do to make it more fun? What do you do to make your coworkers' jobs fun as well?

Sample Behaviors for This Value

* Turns the ordinary into something extraordinary
* Has an authentic sense of self
* Lets their inner quirkiness come out

No. 4. Be Adventurous, Creative, and Open-Minded

At Zappos, we think it's important for people and the company as a whole to be bold and daring (but not reckless). We want everyone to not be afraid to take risks and to not be afraid to make mistakes, because if people aren't making mistakes then that means they're not taking enough risks. Over time, we want everyone to develop his/her gut about business decisions.

We want people to develop and improve their decision-making skills. We encourage people to make mistakes as long as they learn from them. We never want to become complacent and accept the status quo just because that's the way things have always been done. We should always be seeking adventure and having fun exploring new possibilities. By having the freedom to be creative in our solutions, we end up making our own luck. We approach situations and challenges with an open mind. Sometimes our sense of adventure and creativity causes us to be unconventional in our solutions (because we have the freedom to think outside the box), but that's what allows us to rise above and stay ahead of the competition.

Ask Yourself: Are you taking enough risks? Are you afraid of making mistakes? Do you push yourself outside of your comfort zone? Is there a sense of adventure and creativity in the work that you do? What are some creative things that you can contribute to Zappos? Do you approach situations and challenges with an open mind?

Sample Behaviors for This Value

* Unafraid of taking risks.
* Thinks even bigger.
* Is willing to fail (and learn from failure).
* Acts as an entrepreneur.
* Makes the best decisions for their role/work to support their circle's purpose and the company's purpose. Money, while it should be considered, is not a deciding factor.

No. 5. Pursue Growth and Learning

At Zappos, we think it's important for employees to grow both personally and professionally. It's important to constantly challenge and stretch yourself, and not be stuck in a job where you don't feel like you are growing or learning. We believe that inside every employee is more potential than even the employee himself/herself realizes. Our goal is to help employees unlock that potential.

But it has to be a joint effort: You have to want to challenge and stretch yourself for it to happen. If you've been at Zappos for more than a few months, one thing is clear: Zappos is growing. We grow because we take on new challenges, and we face even more new challenges because we're growing. It's an endless cycle, and it's a good thing: It's the only way for a company to survive.

But it can also at times feel risky, stressful, and confusing. Sometimes it may seem that new problems crop up as fast as we solve the old ones (sometimes faster!), but that just means that we're moving—that we're getting better and stronger. Anyone who wants to compete with us has to learn the same things, so problems are just mile markers. Each one we pass means we've gotten better. Yet no matter how much better we get, we'll always have hard work to do, we'll never be done, and we'll never "get it right."

That may seem negative, but it's not: We'll do our best to "get it right," and then do it again when we find out that things have changed. That is the cycle of growth, and like it or not, that cycle won't stop. It's hard . . . but if we weren't doing something hard, then we'd have no business. The only reason we aren't swamped by our competition is because what we do is hard, and we do it better than anyone else. If it ever gets too easy, start looking for a tidal wave of competition to wash us away. It may seem sometimes like we don't know what we're doing. And it's true: We don't. That's a bit scary, but you can take comfort in knowing that nobody else knows how to do what we're doing either. If they did, they'd be the web's most popular shoe store. Sure, people have done parts of what we do before, but what we've learned over the years at Zappos is that the devil is in the details. And that's where we're breaking new ground.

So there are no experts in what we're doing. Except for us: We are becoming experts as we do this. And for anyone we bring on board, the best expertise they can bring is expertise at learning and adapting and figuring new things out—helping the company grow, and in the process they will also be growing themselves.

Ask Yourself: How do you grow personally? How do you grow professionally? Are you a better person today than you were yesterday? How do you get your fellow circle members to grow personally? How do you get your fellow circle members to grow professionally? How do you challenge and stretch yourself? Are you learning something every day? What is your vision for where you want to go? How do you get the company as a whole to grow? Are you doing everything you can to promote company growth, and at the same time are you helping others understand the growth? Do you understand the company purpose? Do you understand the purpose of your circle?

Sample Behaviors for This Value

* Is curious about how things work
* Has insatiable appetite for improvement
* Is their own teacher (self-evaluative)
* Inspires and mentors each other

No. 6. Build Open and Honest Relationships with Communication

Fundamentally, we believe that openness and honesty make for the best relationships because that leads to trust and faith. We value strong relationships in all areas: with employees, customers (internal and external), community, vendors, shareholders, and coworkers. Strong, positive relationships that are open and honest are a big part of what differentiates Zappos from most other companies. Strong relationships allow us to accomplish much more than we would be able to otherwise.

A key ingredient in strong relationships is to develop emotional connections. It's important to always act with integrity in your relationships, to be compassionate, friendly, and loyal, and to make sure that you do the right thing and treat your relationships well. The hardest thing to do is to build trust, but if the trust exists, you can accomplish so much more. In any relationship, it's important to be a good listener as well as a good communicator. Open, honest communication is the best foundation for any relationship, but remember that at the end of the day it's not what you say or what you do, but how you make people feel that matters the most. For someone to feel good about a relationship, he/she must know that the other person truly cares about them, both personally and professionally.

At Zappos, we embrace diversity in thoughts, opinions, and backgrounds. The more widespread and diverse your relationships are, the bigger the positive impact you can make on the company, and the more valuable you will be to the company. It is critical for relationship building to have effective, open, and honest communication. As the company grows, communication becomes more and more important, because everyone needs to understand how his/her team connects to the big picture of what we're trying to accomplish. Communication is always one of the weakest spots in any organization, no matter how good the communication is. We want everyone to always try to go the extra mile in encouraging thorough, complete, and effective communication.

Ask Yourself: How much do people enjoy working with you? How can you improve those relationships? What new relationships can you build throughout the company beyond just the coworkers that you work with on a daily basis? How do you WOW the people that you have relationships with? How can you make your relationships more open and honest? How can you do a better job of communicating with everyone?

Sample Behaviors for This Value

* Wants to hear ideas/input from others
* Is transparent about both positive and negative information
* Connects people to sort out differences
* Agrees to process their tensions, prioritize their work, in short; play by the rules of Holacracy, follows the constitution, and enacts it as best they can

No. 7. Build a Positive Team and Family Spirit

At Zappos, we place a lot of emphasis on our culture because we are both a team and a family. We want to create an environment that is friendly, warm, and exciting. We encourage diversity in ideas, opinions, and points of view. The best leaders are those that lead by example and are both team followers as well as team leaders. We believe that in general, the best ideas and decisions can come from the bottom up, meaning by those on the front lines that are closest to the issues and/or the customers. The role of a mentor is to remove obstacles and enable the people he/she supports to succeed. This means the best leaders are servant-leaders. They serve those they lead.

The best team members take initiative when they notice issues so that the team and the company can succeed. The best team members take ownership of issues and collaborate with other team members whenever challenges arise. The best team members have a positive influence on one another and everyone they encounter. They strive to eliminate any kind of cynicism and negative interactions. Instead, the best team members are those that strive to create harmony with each other and whoever else they interact with.

We believe that the best teams are those that not only work with each other, but also interact with each other outside the office environment. Many of the company's best ideas have been the direct result of informal interactions—for example, the

THE OATH OF EMPLOYMENT   243

idea for our culture book came about from a casual discussion outside the office. We are more than just a team, though—we are a family. We watch out for each other, care for each other, and go above and beyond for each other because we believe in each other and we trust each other. We work together but we also play together. Our bonds go far beyond the typical "coworker" relationships found at most other companies.

Ask Yourself: How do you encourage more teamwork? How do you encourage more people to take initiative? How do you encourage more people to take ownership? What can you do with your team members so that you feel both like a family and a team? How can you build stronger relationships with your team members both inside and outside the office? Do you instill a sense of team and family not just within your department, but across the entire company? Do you exemplify a positive team spirit?

Sample Behaviors for This Value

* Is more than just a coworker
* Connects people for meaningful relationships
* "When I think of the team, I think of them"
* Participates in company-sponsored events (target is 20% of the time/events)
* Is visible to coworkers
* Leads by example, walks the talk

No. 8. Do More with Less

Zappos has always been about being able to do more with less. While we may be casual in our interactions with each other, we are focused and serious about the operations of our business. We believe in hard work and putting in the extra effort to get things done. We believe in operational excellence and realize that there is always room for improvement in everything we do.

This means that our work is never done. To stay ahead of the competition (or would-be competition), we need to continuously innovate as well as make incremental improvements to our operations, always striving to make ourselves more efficient, always trying to figure out how to do something better. We use mistakes as learning opportunities. We must never lose our sense of urgency in making improvements. We must never settle for "good enough," because good is the enemy of great, and our goal is to not only become a great company, but to become the greatest service company in the world. We set and exceed our own high standards, constantly raising the bar for competitors and for ourselves.

Ask Yourself: How can you do what you're doing more efficiently? How can your department become more efficient? How can the company as a whole become more efficient? How can you personally help the company become more efficient?

Sample Behaviors for This Value

* Is MacGyver? Just give me some duct tape!
* Gets sh!t done with less
* "Just do it" attitude (values hard work)
* Completes eight hours of phone time, helping our customers during the holidays (Holiday Helper hours)

No. 9. Be Passionate and Determined

Passion is the fuel that drives ourselves and our company forward. We value passion, determination, perseverance, and the sense of urgency. We are inspired because we believe in what we are doing and where we are going. We don't take "no" or "that'll never work" for an answer, because if we had, Zappos would never have started in the first place. Passion and determination are contagious. We believe in having a positive and optimistic (but realistic) attitude about everything we do, because we realize that this inspires others to have the same attitude. There is excitement in knowing that everyone you work with has a tremendous impact on a larger dream and vision, and you can see that impact day in and day out.

Ask Yourself: Are you passionate about the company? Are you passionate about your work? Do you love what you do and who you work with? Are you happy here? Are you inspired? Do you believe in what we are doing and where we are going? Is this the place for you?

Sample Behaviors for This Value

* Asks for forgiveness, not for permission
* Never believes the statement "It can't be done"
* Fights the fight if it's the right thing for our vision
* Makes decisions based on our core values and value our culture above all else
* Protects the Zappos culture
* Acts in service of the internal board purpose as noted in GlassFrog
* Supports and energizes our 4Cs: clothing, customer service, company culture, and community

No. 10. Be Humble

While we have grown quickly in the past, we recognize that there are always challenges ahead to tackle. We believe that no matter what happens, we should always be respectful of everyone. While we celebrate our individual and team successes, we are not arrogant nor do we treat others differently from how we would want to be treated. Instead, we carry ourselves with a quiet confidence, because we believe that in the long run our character will speak for itself.

Ask Yourself: Are you humble when talking about your accomplishments? Are you humble when talking about the company's accomplishments? Do you treat both large and small vendors with the same amount of respect that they treat you?

Sample Behaviors for This Value

* Displays a quiet confidence for their achievements
* Takes responsibility and admits mistakes
* Listens before being heard

ACKNOWLEDGMENTS

It takes a village to publish a book. This project would not have been possible without the help of so many passionate individuals, teams, and companies who have worked incredibly hard to help us make this idea a reality over the last couple of years.

Thank you to all of the folks in the publishing industry who took a chance on us and were open-minded about doing something different. Thank you to Glenn Yeffeth and the rest of our publishing partners at BenBella Books for taking a chance on our project. We couldn't have picked a better publisher in the end. This book is unlike any other business book out there and we thank you for taking a huge leap of faith. It's been such a rewarding journey taking this risk together. Your team is breaking the mold in the industry and we can't wait to see where it leads next. A huge thank-you in particular goes out to a few folks: our incredible editor, Vy Tran, for your mind, expertise, and passion throughout all of this. You've taught us so much and have strengthened this book from the inside out. To Sarah Avinger, Jessika Rieck, and Kit Sweeney for your incredible patience and art direction guiding us to make this a beautiful book. To Jennifer Canzoneri for your fierce marketing skills. And to Alicia Kania, Adrienne Lang, Rachel Phares, Susan Welte, and Leah Wilson, and the rest of the team for all of your incredible contributions to streamline this entire experience.

Another huge thank-you goes out to our Zappos CEO, Tony Hsieh. It was mere serendipity that led to your strange question, "How much would you charge to produce a book?" . . . that led to a conversation . . . which led to a pitch . . . finally leading to this eventual book, and our team couldn't be more grateful to have had the opportunity to work on this project. Your trust and belief in not just us but each and every Zapponian is incredibly inspiring. You are true to your word. You empower each and every one of us to make this company better and better without dictating what that has to look like.

A huge thank-you as well to our internal supporters, who have granted us the trust and resources to make this book happen. Arun Rajan and Joseph Grusman, thank you for taking the initial chance on our team. It's been a longer journey than anticipated, but we are so thrilled to have had your support over the years. Tyler Williams, you are amazing and having your trust over the years has been immensely appreciated through and through. Chris Peake, we are so grateful to have you by our side as our cheerleader and adviser as we venture into the world of Market-Based Dynamics.

Thank you times a million to Christa Foley—our Head of Brand Vision, Head of Talent Acquisition, and Head of External Culture Training. Thank you for your blood, sweat, and tears. Well . . . hopefully not blood. But thank you so much for everything in this sprint to the finish line as we pulled you in deeper to this project than planned or expected. Thank you for pushing our thinking and providing us the insight we need to strengthen this book at its core. You are amazing.

Thank you to our fellow Zapponians for being a part of this story. While we couldn't include literally every employee's story and interview (though we wanted to), each and every one of you—current, former, and future employees—are as much an integral part of this story as the next person. A special thank-you to each and every individual who trusted us with their time and testimony along the way: Steven Bautista, Loren Becker, Jovahn Bergeron, Johnnie Brockett, Rachael Brown, John Bunch, Saul Dave, Hollie Delaney, Debra De Leon, Jeff Espersen, Ned Farra, Christa Foley, Kelli Frantik, Jim Green, Joe Grusman, Derrin Hawkins, Miguel Hernandez, Audrea Hooper, Tony Hsieh, Stephanie Hudec, Aki Iida, Katrina Jadkowski, Jesse Juhala, Scott Julian, Molly Kettle, John Krikorian, Tiani Lee-Manaois, Jeff Lewis, Maritza Lewis, Jeanne Markel, Chris Mattice, Teri McNally, Veronica Montanez, Stephanie Mora, Rachel Murch, Andre Narcesse, Jamie Naughton, Mike Normart, Daniel Oakley, Lauren Pappert, Jamie Parham, Chris Peake, Megan Petrini, Bhawna Provenzano, Arun Rajan, Regina Renda, Rob Siefker, Kelly Smith, Eileen Tetreault, Matt Thomas, Cindy Toledo, James Van Buren, Stephanie Van Hasselt, McKendree Walker, Susan Walker, Joseph Patrick Warren, Tyler Williams, Dana Zumbo, Tia Zuniga, and Ryo Zsun. We're sorry if anyone was left out!

An extra thank-you to Darrin Caldwell, Peter Gaunt, and Derrin Hawkins for your art direction and creative masterminds to visually bring this book to life.

Thank you to our legal, PR, and finance teams for your long hours and hard work on this project: Kristina Broumand, Joanna Hass, Ingrid Llewellyn, John Murphy, Jamie Naughton, Scott Schaefer, and Jennifer Schmeling. You all are the backbone to every project and protectors of our brand. Thank you to Kristen Chasseur, Jeanne Markel, and all of our wonderful ninjas who were helpful in the logistics behind the making of this book. Thank you from the bottom of our hearts to our brands, vendors, partners, and community that has surrounded Zappos with so much love and support over the years. Thank you to the city of Las Vegas for allowing us to call it home. This city has so much pride and we are so grateful to be a small part of this wonderful place.

Thank you to our dearest Zappos customers and fans who've stuck by our side for the last twenty years. You make us strive to be better and better. You are the center of Zappos and all that we do. Without you, there is no us and we thank you very much for that. Thank you to our partners at Amazon for supporting and believing in the culture here at Zappos.

We also need to thank our partners and agents at Aevitas Creative Management for taking this risk with us, and a few, in particular, who have been incredibly helpful along the way: Justin Brouckaert, Shenel Ekici-Moling, Erin Files, Chelsey Heller, David Kuhn, Sarah Levitt, and Todd Shuster.

Above all, our deepest gratitude goes out to Mark Dagostino and his agent, Madeleine Morel. Madeleine, you were an incredible adviser and liaison throughout this whole project. Mark, little did we know that we would be taking this two-year journey when we first connected. But here we are—we did it! It's been a labor of love and so incredibly rewarding. We owe a huge, huge thank-you to you for your time, energy, optimism, writing, travels, and good company you've given us over the years. You've not only been an amazing partner and mind to have by our side but you've become a close friend to us and part of our very own Zappos family. We love you!

And last, but surely not least, thank you to you . . . yes, you! Our lovely reader—especially if you got this far. Keep taking risks in everything you do. Chase those challenges with your service foot forward. There's an opportunity on the other side of every "yes." That rings true whether it's in business or in life.

Derrin Hawkins
Kelly Smith
Tia Zuniga
Zappos THINK team

ABOUT
THE AUTHORS

 **ZAPPOS.COM** is a customer service company that just happens to sell shoes, clothing, and accessories online. Known for its Ten Core Values and unique organizational structure, Zappos approaches hiring and recruiting in a way that is both highly selective and meticulously focused on finding candidates who will make customers say "WOW." The employees of Zappos (Zapponians, as they're called) make everyday business decisions with one eye focused on the resilience of their culture. The stories compiled in *The Power of WOW* offer a behind-the-scenes look into the evolution of a service-obsessed brand and how it plans to continue delivering happiness for the next 500 years.

 At the age of twenty-four, **TONY HSIEH** joined Zappos as an adviser and investor, eventually becoming CEO and helping Zappos grow from almost no sales to a multibillion-dollar company dedicated to customer service, company culture, and community. Tony is also the author of the #1 *New York Times* bestseller *Delivering Happiness*. Residence: Las Vegas, NV.

 Dedicated to writing books that inspire and uplift, **MARK DAGOSTINO** is a #1 *New York Times* bestselling coauthor and former senior writer for *People* magazine. He has appeared as a celebrity expert on CNN, *Today*, *The Early Show*, *The View*, *Inside Edition*, *Entertainment Tonight*, and dozens of other national TV shows. Residence: Stratham, NH.

Success Comes With Company Culture...
Welcome to Zappos Insights!

Zappos Insights is a team within Zappos.com who love teaching other companies about how to improve their culture, attract and keep great people, deliver exceptional customer service, and grow their business. Culture is totally our jam here at Zappos and Zappos Insights.

You might know a bit about Tony's story, that he started his first company in college and ultimately wound up selling it. But what a lot of people don't know is that he sold it because he wasn't happy going to work there anymore, because it didn't align with his values, and it wasn't fun anymore for him. In short, a set of core values by which his company operated had not been identified and, therefore, the culture of the organization shifted to something he didn't like.

At Zappos, we've been talking about the importance of company culture since 2004. Tony wrote about it in his book *Delivering Happiness*. And through our history, what we've learned is that company culture IS what makes the difference between success and failure. It's what helped us grow our business, our profit, deliver exceptional customer service, retain our talent, and have fun along the way.

We know that if you identify your company's core values, hire by them, onboard team members by them, and truly live them, then you can get out of the way, and your team will do the best job for you and your customers.

People frequently ask us what the ROI of culture is. I think Tony has the best reply to this: "Just because you can't measure the ROI of something doesn't mean you shouldn't do it. What's the ROI on hugging your mom?"

I salute you for caring about your company's culture, your people, and your customers. And I invite you to explore the ways Zappos Insights can help you in your journey to being the best company you can be.

Learn more at https://www.zps.to/pow

Christa Foley

Head of Brand Vision
Head of Talent Acquisition
Head of External Culture Training